NEW ORLEANS

Classic

SEAFOOD

NEW ORLEANS

classic

SEAFOOD

Recipes from Favorite Restaurants

KIT WOHL

PELICAN PUBLISHING COMPANY

GRETNA 2008

The word "Pelican" and the depiction of a pelican are trademarks
of Pelican Publishing Company, Inc., and are registered in the
U.S. Patent and Trademark Office.

ISBN 978-1-58980-516-3

Edited by Lloyd Dobyns and Michele Vine

Printed in Singapore
Published by Pelican Publishing Company, Inc.
1000 Burmaster Street, Gretna, Louisiana 70053

FOR MY CHERISHED SISTERS AND BROTHERS,
NIECES, AND NEPHEWS. REMEMBER THE MEALS.

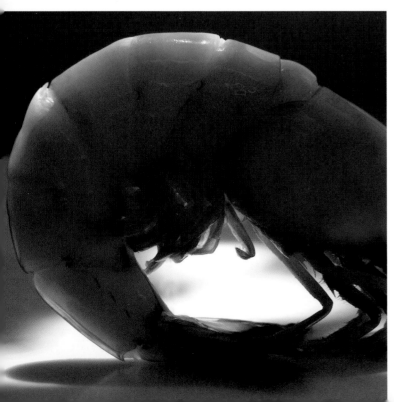

CONTENTS

FINFISH

Chapter V FISH & SEAFOOD COMBOS

Chapter VI SEASONINGS

INTRODUCTION

"IF IT SWIMS, WE'LL PROBABLY EAT IT."

New Orleans is surrounded by water. In fact, it is below sea level – so low that seafood could jump from their natural habitat right onto our plates, if inclined. But we're happy to give the seafood a hand up. And no hurricane is ever going to change that.

A day at the lake, or by a bayou, or sitting on the riverbank with a line in the water: glory. If there are a few fishing poles and crab nets in the garage, you're probably a local. You also own a crawfish pot or two and propane burner rig. Some workers, when hired, announce that they will not be available during fishing season. This is not a deal-breaker as long as fresh fish is offered in return. As you can imagine, boat owners are very popular here, too. Face it; most Orleanians are natural born seafood aficionados. I do know one gentleman who wasn't, but he moved.

Maybe it was the mudbugs.

You can call them crawfish if you prefer, but never call them crayfish. And respect those little suckers. We do. Mudbugs will sometimes sashay in a crawfish chorus line across a road from one bayou to another. Hundreds of them. When this happens, traffic stops; people either allow them to pass, or jump from their vehicles, and scoop them up.

Then there are those special times of the year when crawfish, shrimp, and crabs are in season together. We rejoice in backyards and parks. We roll up our sleeves, cover a table with black garbage bags topped by several layers of newspaper, and wait. The results, boiled in a huge pot, are drained and piled on the table. The rules are simple; there's nothing dainty about the process. He who eats the fastest gets the most. Actually, unless you can quickly peel shrimp and crawfish – and crack crabs at warp speed – you could starve to death around these parts. That's why we add potatoes, corn, sausage, and other nice things to the pot.

One afternoon a bunch of us had loaded the table at local seafood joint (everybody has a favorite neighborhood one-step-above-a-dive fish house. Mine is Franky and Johnny's) with a three-crustation boil. Visitors – tourists, probably – seated at the next table watched as our arms flew and hands flailed, dismembering small creatures whose small parts also flailed and flew. Not a knife or fork in sight. Just smackin' and smilin'.

"Ewwww, gross," said one of the ladies at the tourist table. We all felt sorry for her. She just didn't get it.

And, bless her heart; she never knew what she was missing.

On to oysters. Raw oysters here are so fresh you taste the Gulf of Mexico before you taste the oyster. Or maybe they're the same thing. Prepare your own cocktail sauce, at the table or bar, and then spend some appetite eating them on the half shell. Again, you don't need a fork when a correctly shucked oyster will practically slide out of its shell and into your mouth all by itself.

Great seafood here can be just that simple.

Or it can get dressed up in fancy duds and ready to party.

Famous restaurants, uptown, downtown, and back of town daily elevate fish and shellfish from basic boiled beauties to traditional (and untraditional) classics. Catfish can make you sob. Soft shell crabs seem like crispy clouds. Speckled trout, shrimp, pompano, and redfish come blackened, broiled, grilled, sautéed, steamed, sauced and sassy as all get out. Put another way, when it comes to seafood, we Orleanians like to swing all ways. The recipes in this book demonstrate how the low, the high, and the mighty buoyantly co-exist in a dining world that ranges from blue jeans to black tie. With taste buds to match.

Of course, there's a difference between what a restaurant serves, and making your own. Restaurant chefs have experience, knowledge, and special tricks. No matter. These recipes aren't written for the professional, although they may make you look like one. Each dish has been home-kitchen tested by real people who are not chefs in real life. We want you to be happy, look good, and be able to duplicate a famous recipe simply and easily right in your own backyard.

Or kitchen.

A final note. If handling fresh fish makes you squeamish, remember what a native Orleanian, and a pretty picky eater herself, once told me: At least seafood doesn't have eyelashes.

– Kit Wohl

CRABS

Applause embarrasses a blue crab so much that when it is caught and boiled it turns bright red.

Joy is a pile of boiled Louisiana blue crabs. In other places savvy folks have discovered the superiority of Louisiana blue crabs and now demand that they be shared and shipped around the country. When there is a shortage, I take this shipping-sharing thing personally. I want to keep them home. Preferably at my house.

Fine crabmeat has a fresh, delicate flavor reminiscent of the waters where the crabs grew up, and around New Orleans, that's almost buttery. That's why we try to do as little as possible to crabmeat, enhancing rather than overpowering its natural flavor.

Crabs live in hard, protective shells except at a certain time of the year when crabs abandon the old houses and build larger, new houses, which harden quickly. That's when soft-shell crabs are in season and another reason to head to a favorite restaurant, to the nearest fish market, or to the end of the dock with a chicken neck and net to go crabbing. Fried or sautéed soft-shell crabs are the stars at most tables. People allergic to crabmeat should sit next to me at dinner.

Crabs are sold live, boiled, or steamed. They are purchased whole, graded by size, or as pure crabmeat picked by a noble person. Do pick through the crabmeat carefully, to catch the bits of shell and cartilage that the official picker may have missed. The containers will be labeled jumbo, special, or claws and fingers.

Rarely seen, but greatly appreciated are small buster crabs. There are old-time crab farmers who catch the tiny crabs and place them in large tanks. There they stay, swimming with the farmer watching as a benevolent life guard until they shed their hard shell. These babies, gently sautéed in a classic meunière sauce and served on a piece of buttered toast can make the most blasé guest beg like a puppy.

We prefer the seasoning mixture known as crab boil, which we also use for shrimp and crawfish.

Anything else tastes funny to us.

© Photograph Donn Young

CRAB BISQUE

Straight from the dock at hunting camp comes crab bisque with finesse and flavor. The beauty of the bisque is its subtle richness that doesn't overwhelm the delicate crabmeat. I prefer the jumbo lump, as opposed to the smaller grades of crabmeat because it is a luxurious dish and should be treated as a special occasion. This recipe provides 6 servings, but the same quantity and richness would serve 12 in demitasse cups as a lovely starter.

SERVES: 6

1/4 cup	unsalted butter		1 pint	heavy cream
3 tablespoons	all-purpose flour		1 teaspoon	thyme, finely chopped
1 pound	jumbo crabmeat		1 teaspoon	kosher salt
3 tablespoons	onions, finely chopped		1/8 teaspoon	white pepper
1 tablespoon	celery, finely chopped		1/8 teaspoon	cayenne pepper
1 quart	whole milk		1/4 cup	parsley, chopped

DIRECTIONS

Clean the crabmeat carefully to remove any remaining shell or cartilage. Be careful not to break the lumps. Reserve 6 jumbo lumps as garnish for each serving.

Make a blond roux by melting the butter and gradually stirring in the flour over a medium heat. Lower the heat if it seems to be turning color. Stir continuously and do not allow the mixture to brown, about 5-10 minutes.

Add the onions and celery. Cook, continuing to stir, until the onions are translucent, about 5-10 minutes.

Gradually add the milk and cream, stirring constantly, and continue to cook as it thickens. Add thyme, salt, pepper, and cayenne. Taste and adjust seasonings as desired. Carefully add crabmeat to the bisque and allow the crabmeat to warm through, about 2 minutes. In a small sauté pan, warm the reserved jumbo lumps and set aside.

For garnish, sprinkle with chopped parsley and float a large piece of jumbo lump on top.

Marti Shambra was passionate about top hats and tall tales, and he held forth of any manner of subjects from design to designing escapades as an artist and social creature, attracting literati, the theater crowd, Quarterites, and the media people. He adored delicious gossip and snacked on adversaries.

He ruled Marti's, the first of the French Quarter bistros that provided a snappy, late night, casual hangout for the locals, one of whom was Tennessee Williams. He lived around the corner and was unnoticed or, at least, undisturbed by other guests. Marti's suited him.

Marti Shambra was far more interested in maintaining a salon than cooking but he demanded a good menu, so he wisely installed his family's hunting-camp cook in the kitchen and left him alone. He got wonderful food and great conversation.

Chef Henry Robinson presented solid fare. It was simple, down-home goodness. There was nothing tricky, nothing fancy, nothing tortured into unnatural culinary acts. I usually started with the crab bisque if it was on the daily special blackboard.

Following Marti's too-early passing in 1988, the bistro was renamed Peristyle, after the bar's mural of City Park, circa 1911, from the old DeSoto Hotel and continues to be an acclaimed establishment.

PALACE CAFE
CRABMEAT CHEESECAKE

This recipe is so richly divine that you may want to consider serving it as an appetizer in small slices. On the other hand, your guests may fight over the scraps so perhaps it should be served as a whole piece.

SERVES: 8

PECAN CRUST

3/4 cup	pecans
1 cup	all-purpose flour
1/4 teaspoon	salt
5 tablespoons	cold butter
3 tablespoons	ice water

CRABMEAT FILLING

1/2 cup	onions, small diced
1 tablespoon	butter
4 ounces	crabmeat
8 ounces	cream cheese, room temperature
1/3 cup	Creole cream cheese or sour cream
2 large	eggs
1 tablespoon	Tabasco™ sauce
to taste	kosher salt and cracked white pepper

MEUNIÈRE SAUCE

1	lemon, peeled and quartered
1/2 cup	Worcestershire sauce
1/2 cup	Tabasco™ sauce
1/4 cup	heavy whipping cream
1 pound	cold butter, cut into cubes
to taste	kosher salt and cracked white pepper

GARNISH

2 cups	sliced mixed wild mushrooms
3 tablespoons	butter, softened
24	crab claw fingers
to taste	kosher salt and cracked black pepper

DIRECTIONS

Preheat oven to 350°F. Finely grind pecans in a food processor. Add flour and salt. Mix well. Transfer to a large mixing bowl and cut butter into flour with two knives until dough is in crumbs the size of small peas. Add ice water and evenly incorporate into the dough, which should remain fairly crumbly. Roll out dough to 1/8 inch thickness on a lightly floured surface. Press dough into a lightly greased 9-inch tart pan, starting with the sides and then the bottom. Bake crust for 20 minutes, or until golden brown. Reset oven to 300°F.

Note: Dough can be made ahead of time. If doing so, wrap the dough tightly in plastic wrap and refrigerate. Allow dough to come to room temperature before rolling it out.

Sauté onions in butter until translucent. Add crabmeat and cook just until heated through, then remove from heat. Blend cream cheese until smooth in a mixer fitted with a paddle, or by hand using a wooden spoon. Add Creole cream cheese and mix well. Mix in the eggs one at a time. Gently fold in crabmeat mixture. Stir in Tabasco sauce and season to taste with salt and cracked white pepper. Spoon filling into prepared crust. Bake at 300°F for 30-40 minutes, or until firm to the touch.

Prepare the meunière sauce and garnish. To serve, slice cheesecake and top each piece with warm meunière sauce and three crab claws.

Following his family's ever-expanding restaurant tradition, Dickie Brennan has used his Palace Café to create dishes destined to become New Orleans' classics. He also created Dickie Brennan's Steakhouse and Dickie Brennan's Bourbon House. In it's first year Esquire Magazine named it one of the country's top ten restaurants. Many accolades and awards have followed.

Prior to retirement, his father Dick Brennan presided over Commander's Palace with his sisters, Ella Brennan and Dottie Brennan, each bringing their own talents to the table and grooming this generation of Brennans.

Dickie has done his family proud by continuing their commitment to culinary and community excellence.

MEUNIÈRE SAUCE AND GARNISH

Combine lemon, Worcestershire sauce, and Tabasco™ sauce in a heavy saucepot. Reduce over medium heat, stirring constantly with a wire whisk until mixture becomes thick and syrupy. Whisk in heavy whipping cream. Reduce heat to low and slowly blend in butter one cube at a time, only after previously added butter has been completely incorporated into the sauce. Remove from heat and continue to stir. Season with salt and cracked pepper to taste. Strain through a fine strainer and keep warm. Sauté mushrooms in 2 tablespoons of butter until tender and all moisture has cooked off. Excess water from the mushrooms may cause your sauce to separate if it isn't cooked off. Stir mushrooms into meunière sauce. Melt 1 tablespoon of butter in a sauté pan and warm crab claws over low heat.

GALATOIRE'S

CRABMEAT MAISON

Crabmeat Maison at Galatoire's is their version of Crabmeat Ravigotte. The big difference is jumbo lumps of crabmeat, the service, and of course, the surroundings. Maison means house and the house specialty it is, indeed.

SERVES: 6

2 large	egg yolks	to taste	salt and freshly ground
2 tablespoons	red wine vinegar		white pepper
1 tablespoon	Creole mustard or any coarse	1 pound	jumbo lump crabmeat
	grainy brown mustard	1 head	iceberg lettuce, washed,
1 teaspoon	fresh lemon juice		dried and cut into
1 cup	vegetable oil		thin ribbons
1/4 cup	nonpareil capers, drained	2 medium	vine-ripened tomatoes,
1/4 cup	chopped scallions, green and		cored and cut into six
	white parts		1-inch thick slices
1 tablespoon	curly parsley, chopped	garnish	fresh parsley, chopped

DIRECTIONS

Combine the egg yolks, vinegar, mustard, and lemon juice in a food processor and process for 2 minutes. With the processor running, add the oil slowly in a thin stream and process until emulsified. (*Note: it will not completely mix.*)

Transfer to a large mixing bowl and gently fold in the capers, scallions, and parsley. Season with salt and white pepper. Refrigerate for 2 to 4 hours.

Just before serving, gently fold in the crabmeat, taking care not to break the lumps.

Divide the lettuce among 6 serving plates and top with a slice of tomato. Spoon the crabmeat on top of the tomato slices. Garnish with fresh chopped parsley and serve.

MÉLANGE AT THE RITZ-CARLTON
JUMBO LUMP CRAB CAKES

The combination of seasoned crabmeat spiked with piquanté sauce and cooled by fennel slaw is a bodacious surprise of texture and flavor.

SERVES: 6 Appetizers

SAUCE PIQUANTÉ

2 teaspoons	olive oil
1 tablespoon	garlic, chopped
1 tablespoon	jalapeño pepper, seeded and finely chopped
1/4 cup	yellow onions, finely diced
1/4 cup	celery, finely diced
1/4 cup	green bell pepper, finely diced
2 cups	tomato juice
1 sprig	fresh tarragon, chopped
1/2 cup	fresh tomato, medium diced

CRAB CAKES

1/3 cup	red onions, finely diced
1/4 cup	red bell pepper, finely diced
1/4 cup	green bell pepper, finely diced
1/2 cup	mayonnaise
2 teaspoons	Creole mustard
1 teaspoon	prepared horseradish
1 tablespoon	fresh thyme, chopped
1 cup	Italian bread crumbs
1 1/2 pounds	jumbo lump crabmeat
pinch	cayenne pepper
to taste	salt and freshly ground black pepper

FENNEL SLAW

1 cup	fresh fennel bulb, thinly shaved
2 tablespoons	cane vinegar

DIRECTIONS

For the sauce piquanté, heat the olive oil in a 12-inch saucepan over medium heat. Sauté the garlic, jalapeños, onions, celery, and green peppers, about 3-5 minutes. Add the tomato juice and tarragon, reduce heat. Simmer over low heat for 10 minutes. Stir in the diced fresh tomato and heat about 1 minute. Remove from the heat, and set aside.

To create the fennel slaw, toss the thinly shaved fennel bulb with the cane vinegar, and set aside.

Crab cakes must be gently handled to avoid breaking the lumps. Combine the red onions, bell peppers, mayonnaise, mustard, horseradish, fresh thyme, Italian bread crumbs, and mix well. Gently fold in the jumbo lump crabmeat. Add the cayenne pepper, salt, and freshly ground black pepper. Taste and adjust seasonings as desired.

Divide the mixture into six balls. Flatten to make the cakes. In a non-stick skillet over medium heat, sear the crab cakes on both sides, turning once.

Ladle piquanté sauce onto a serving platter or individual plates. Place the crab cakes on top of the sauce and garnish each with 1 or 2 teaspoons of the fennel slaw. Serve immediately.

When The Ritz-Carlton offered a transfer to New Orleans as general manager, Myra deGersdorff came home to where her heart lives, the city where she grew up.

"We need a New Orleans restaurant," she mused. "So why not all of them?" The theme of the hotel's reopening was about celebrating New Orleans food, music and entertainment. To highlight the city's restaurants for guests who want a local taste, it is a natural.

Mélange is pure entertainment. When our most heralded establishments share their recipes to offer their most famous dishes on one menu, it's a coming together of delicious tradition, then the menu is accented by some of The Ritz-Carlton's culinary creations.

Guests get a taste of the city and what restaurant wouldn't want to be featured to a Ritz-Carlton guest?

When the landmark Maison Blanche building, a former department store, was revitalized as a grand hotel, it was serendipity that the antique terra cotta exterior was festooned with lion heads, symbol of The Ritz-Carlton.

Macque choux has Cajun roots. Corn off the cob is the standard, but other ingredients may vary according to taste. Tomatoes and okra may be used, or simply bell peppers and onions. Some cooks add pork, others add butter. Mr. B's adds cream so that it ends up a little like Louisiana creamed corn.

MACQUE CHOUX

2 cups	heavy whipping cream
2 tablespoons	unsalted butter
1/2 small	red onion, diced
1/2 medium	red bell pepper, diced
1/2 medium	green bell pepper, diced
3 ears	fresh corn, kernels only
to taste	kosher salt
to taste	freshly ground black pepper

DIRECTIONS

In a medium saucepan simmer cream over moderately low heat until it is reduced in half, about 20 minutes.

In a 12-inch saucepan melt the butter over moderate heat. Add onions and bell peppers and cook for 3 minutes, stirring occasionally. Add corn kernels and cook for 5 minutes, or until tender.

Add the reduced cream and cook 1 minute. Season with salt and pepper to taste.

Keep warm until ready to serve.

MR. B'S
SOFT-SHELL CRAB WITH MACQUE CHOUX

Mr. B's stands for Brennan's, another mighty offshoot of the restaurant group – the Commander's Palace side of the family, if you're keeping score. Managing Partner Cindy Brennan works closely with Executive Chef Michelle McRaney to provide Creole-style specialties in the French Quarter.

SERVES: 4

4 large	live soft-shell crabs	3/4 teaspoon	granulated garlic
for frying	canola oil	1/2 teaspoon	paprika
2 3/4 cups	all-purpose flour	1/2 teaspoon	chili powder
1/2 cup	corn flour	1/2 teaspoon	white pepper
1/2 cup	cornstarch	2 large	eggs
1/4 cup	cornmeal	1/2 cup	water
1 teaspoon	salt	2 cups	macque choux (see sidebar)
3/4 teaspoon	granulated onions		

DIRECTIONS

Start by preparing the macque choux.

With a pair of kitchen scissors while holding the crab in one hand, cut off face (eyes and mouth). Cut off the little flap at the crab bottom and pull top shell sides up and cut off gills. Puncture the water sack behind the eyes and squeeze to remove water.

Heat enough oil to measure 4-inches deep in a tall, wide heavy pot to 375°F.

In a large bowl combine 3/4 cup all-purpose flour, corn flour, cornstarch, cornmeal, salt, granulated onions, garlic, paprika, chili powder, and white pepper. Mix well and set aside. In a small bowl whisk together eggs with 1/2 cup water, to form an eggwash.

Place the remaining 2 cups flour in a shallow bowl. Dredge each crab in flour, being sure to coat the legs. Dip the dredged crab in the egg wash, letting excess batter drip off. Dredge again in the corn flour mixture and shake off the excess.

Gently drop 2 crabs in the hot oil belly side up. Place a ladle on the belly of each crab and let the crab rest on the bottom of the pan, resting ladle handle against the side of the pan. Fry the crabs until golden brown about 4 minutes, making sure oil returns to 375°F before adding more crabs. Drain the crabs on paper towels. Serve warm over macque choux, belly side up.

MARCELLE BIENVENUE
CRAWFISH BISQUE

Marcelle Bienvenu loves the south Louisiana bayous and waterways almost as much as her passion for its products and cooking them. It is her heritage. She's an all around talented Cajun from St. Martinville, Acadiana's heart. Her accent flavors her comments as much as her garden seasons her creations.

There's no one more appropriate to prepare and serve crawfish bisque than Marcelle. She's been the go-to lady for famous chefs, including Emeril Lagasse, Paul Prudhomme, and worked with Ella Brennan at Commander's Palace even before Paul cooked there. She's an author, commentator, and columnist.

Crawfish bisque is the epitome of crustacean fascination. A silky smooth base laced with fresh crawfish tails and vegetables brings into play all of the Creole and Cajun culinary skills. The glory of a great bisque is the stuffing, encased in the crawfish shell heads. It is not really the head, but the shoulder's shell, so don't wince. A savory stuffing of crawfish, bread, crawfish fat, and seasonings packed into it is prepared and placed into the bisque as a little lagniappe, an extra treat.

Should shells not be available, little balls, or boulettes, of the crawfish stuffing, about a tablespoon, can be placed in the oven to brown and serve the same purpose to float in the bisque or as an hors d'oeuvre. This is the queen of Creole recipes so plan to take your time and enjoy the preparation with a friend or two to help and laugh together.

SERVES: 10-12

BISQUE

1 cup	vegetable oil or butter	4 medium	onions, chopped
2 1/2 pounds	crawfish tails, peeled	4 medium	green bell peppers, seeded and chopped
1 cup	crawfish fat (or 1/2 cup butter)	4 ribs	celery, chopped
2 tablespoons	salt	6 to 8 cups	tepid water
1 tablespoon	cayenne pepper	2 tablespoons	green onions, chopped
2 tablespoons	paprika	2 tablespoons	fresh parsley, chopped
1 1/2 cups	hot water	5 to 8 cups	cooked white rice
4 tablespoons	dark brown roux (see page 80)		

DIRECTIONS

Heat 1/2 cup of the oil in a large, heavy pot or Dutch oven over medium heat. Add the crawfish tails, crawfish fat or butter, salt, cayenne, and paprika. Cook, stirring for 3 minutes. Combine the water and the roux in a small pot over medium heat and stir to blend. Add to the crawfish mixture, cook for 2 minutes, stirring occasionally.

Meanwhile, in another large pot, heat the remaining 1/2 cup oil over medium heat. Add the onions, bell peppers, and celery. Sauté until soft and golden, about 8 minutes. Remove from the heat and add the vegetables to the crawfish mixture. Add 3 to 4 cups of water, stirring to blend. Cook until the mixture thickens, about 2 minutes, stirring occasionally. Reduce the heat to medium-low and add the remaining water. Cook until the bisque is slightly thick, about 15 minutes. It should be the consistency of a thick soup. Add the stuffed crawfish heads, the green onions, and the parsley. Cook for about 5 minutes, stirring gently. Serve over steamed white rice.

STUFFING

1 cup	vegetable oil or butter
3 medium	onions, minced
4 ribs	celery, chopped
4 medium	green bell peppers, seeded, and minced
5 cloves	fresh garlic, minced
1/2 cup	crawfish fat (if available, if not use 1/2 cup butter)
1 1/2 pounds	crawfish tails, peeled
8 to 10 slices	day-old bread, soaked in water and squeezed dry
2 tablespoons	salt
1 tablespoon	freshly ground black pepper
1 tablespoon	cayenne pepper
150	crawfish heads, cleaned
1 cup	unseasoned bread crumbs
1 cup	seasoned bread crumbs

DIRECTIONS

Heat 1/2 cup of the oil or butter in a large, heavy pot over medium heat. Add the onions, celery, bell peppers, and garlic. Sauté the vegetables until they are soft and golden, 8 to 10 minutes. Add the crawfish fat or butter and cook, stirring for 3 minutes. Remove from the heat and set aside. Grind 1 pound of the crawfish tails and the bread together in a meat grinder or food processor.

Heat the remaining 1/2 cup oil (or butter) in a large, heavy pot or Dutch oven over medium heat. Add the crawfish/bread mixture, the cooked vegetables, salt, black pepper, cayenne, and the remaining 1/2 pound of crawfish tails. Cook, stirring, for 5 to 8 minutes. Remove from the heat and cool to room temperature, stirring it several times as it cools.

Combine the bread crumbs together in a small bowl and set aside. Preheat the oven to 375°F.

Stuff each crawfish head with about 1 tablespoon of the stuffing mixture and place on a large baking sheet. Cover the stuffing in the crawfish heads with a generous amount of the bread crumbs, patting it gently to adhere to the stuffing. Bake until the bread crumbs are lightly golden brown, 15-20 minutes. Remove from the oven and set aside.

Olivier's menu represents five generations of Creole tradition. Executive Chef Armand Olivier III's great-great grandmother Gaudet passed on her recipes through the family's daughters until they reached him through his mother, Mama Cheryl Gaudet Oliver.

Although the family's matriarchs have provided the recipes, the patriarch's have guided the business. Olivier's is owned and operated by Armand Olivier, Jr. and the Olivier family.

The family has been restaurateurs since 1979. The Olivier family prides itself on authentic Creole recipes handed down through the generations. Their location on Decatur Street in the French Quarter is a historic structure. The exposed bricks behind Chef Olivier are as authentic as its cuisine.

OLIVIER'S CREOLE RESTAURANT
CRAWFISH ÉTOUFFÉE

Roux is the magic ingredient behind many Creole dishes. In Creole cooking, the proportions tend to be a matter of personal preference. This recipe is one-to-one but slightly more flour may be added if the roux seems too thin. Roux not only thickens sauces, gravies, and stocks but adds an unmistakable undertone of taste. Put too simply, perhaps, no roux, no Creole.

SERVES: 4

1/2 cup	olive oil		2 toes	garlic, crushed
1/2 cup	all-purpose flour		2 cups	seafood stock
1 large	yellow onion, finely chopped		2	bay leaves
1/2 medium	green bell pepper, chopped		1/4 cup	fresh parsley, chopped
1/2 cup	celery, chopped		16 ounces	crushed tomatoes
1/2 cup	green onions, finely chopped		3 pounds	live crawfish, peeled or
16 ounces	canned tomatoes, chopped		1 pound	crawfish tails, with fat
8 ounces	tomato sauce		2 cups	cooked white rice
to taste	salt and cayenne pepper			

DIRECTIONS

Use a heavy-bottomed skillet, cast iron, or Dutch oven based on the amount of roux needed. These heavy pans will disperse the heat more slowly and evenly. Plan the time carefully, once a roux has been started it must be attended and constantly stirred. This recipe calls for a medium roux, the color of peanut butter, which takes about 15-25 minutes. Do not allow the mixture to sit on the sides or bottom of the pan. Be careful stirring. Hot splatters hurt. A burned roux will give a bitter and scorched taste to any dish. If the roux scorches or burns, it must be discarded and done again.

In a heavy-bottomed sauce pan add the olive oil over low heat. Slowly add the flour, stir constantly until the flour has been absorbed. As it is stirred, the texture will change, finally becoming a foamy mixture. Continue stirring until it has reached the desired color, medium brown. Take your time.

Add the onions, bell pepper, celery, and green onions to the saucepan. Allow to cook for about 10-15 minutes, or until the onions are clear or translucent.

Add the crushed tomatoes and tomato sauce, mix well. Add the garlic, salt, pepper, seafood stock and cook for about 2-3 minutes. Add the bay leaves and parsley. Cook sauce for 20-25 minutes.

Increase heat to medium, add the Louisiana crawfish tails to the sauce, and cook for an additional 10 minutes.

Serve over cooked white rice. (*See recipe page 50.*)

Garnish with fresh okra, colorful bell peppers, lemon, and parsley if desired.

FRANKY & JOHNNY'S
CRAWFISH PIE

Crawfish pie is one of those magical things to do with leftovers or already picked crawfish from the seafood market. It's a meal, a hand-held lunch, or cocktail party appetizers. In fact, a regular 8-or-9 inch pie would be a spectacular presentation. There's no good reason not to substitute shrimp if Louisiana crawfish are out of season.

SERVES: 12 individual pies or 48 bite-sized canapes

PIE FILLING

2 tablespoons	unsalted butter
1 cup	green onions, thinly sliced
1 stalk	celery, finely chopped
4 cloves	garlic, minced
1 teaspoon	grated lemon rind
1 teaspoon	Tabasco™ sauce
1/2 cup	white wine or water
1 teaspoon	salt-free cajun seasoning
1 pound	crawfish tails
4 ounces	cream cheese, cut into 8 pieces

THE CRUST

3 sheets	frozen puff pastry, thawed
egg wash	1 egg and 1 tablespoon cold water, beaten with fork
Optional	12 prepared tarts shells or 48 bite-sized tart shells

DIRECTIONS

Place the crawfish tails in a strainer to remove any excess water. Thaw the frozen puffed pastry according to the package instructions.

In a large saucepan melt the butter over medium heat. Add the green onions and celery, sauté for about 3 minutes. Add the minced garlic and cook for approximately 2 more minutes or until the vegetables are softened. Add the lemon zest, Tabasco™ sauce, white wine or water, and Cajun seasoning. Stir well, bring to a simmer, and add the crawfish tails. Cook the mixture briefly, to warm the tails. Add the cream cheese and stir until the cheese has melted.

Remove the completed filling from the heat and allow it to cool to room temperature. Meanwhile, preheat the oven to 375°F.

On a lightly floured surface, roll out the pastry to about 1/8 inch thickness. Using a 4-inch plate as a guide, trace and cut out circles. Each sheet should yield 4 circles. You may want to purchase an extra pastry sheet to be certain you have enough for 12 pies. Transfer the circles onto 2 parchment-lined baking sheets. Place a heaping tablespoon of filling on one side of each dough circle. Brush egg wash around the outer edge, then fold the dough over to enclose the filling and press with the tines of a fork or your fingers. Be sure to seal each pie completely. Bake the pies in the oven for 15-20 minutes until golden brown.

A prepared open 8-9 inch tart shell is an alternate presentation. Simply fill the shell to brimming with the crawfish mixture. Bake in a 375°F oven for 15 to 20 minutes until golden brown.

Here's an up-front fact: Franky & Johnny's is my favorite corner seafood joint. The tables and chairs don't match, but are you going to eat the tables and chairs? This is not to criticize your favorite corner joint, only to declare my open prejudice. It's where I take out-of-town guests for local color and great seafood.

Imagine a meal that begins with trays of boiled crawfish and shrimp, side by side with a stuffed artichoke and onions rings. Then the main course – in my case, a platter of fried shrimp, oysters, softshell crab, and catfish.

Occasionally we'll indulge in bites of a crawfish pie or a hot sausage po' boy, so spicy the top of your head will sweat.

Don't let the overhead television set get in your way, and if you get bored, there's the old-fashioned claw machine so you can fish for stuffed animals and other small toys, after you drop some coins in. Have you ever won? Me neither.

George and Darryl Cortello, the owners, keep 45s on the juke box, spinning Irma Thomas and Aaron Neville. The Cortellos tell you it's all about neighborhood culture. It's also all about fun. And seafood. My favorite joint.

Oh. Don't know Irma and Aaron? Just don't tell anybody; it'll be OK.

How much is there to say about three indentured chefs who were hanging out on a beach in Hawaii, cooking for a celebrity event, and said the heck with working back home in the corporate kitchen.

"We're serfs," said Gary. "No, we're surfing," corrected Greg. "That's the point," explained Hans. "Enough suits in our lives. We quit," they agreed.

They named themselves the Taste Buds, and the trio went on to max out their credit cards and wield a hammer. That was while they were testing new dishes in their kitchens at home.

Gary Darling, Hans Limburg and Greg Reggio developed Semolina, which took off like crazy. They devised outrageous dishes to match their personalities; prepared à la minute – at the last minute.

Semolina became so popular that the restaurant grew to several locations. Then they created Zea Rotisserie, another exciting restaurant that continues to expand.

Now Semolina has evolved to embrace Bistro Italia, incorporating Mediterranean style dishes and other culinary escapades.

Will they ever stop? Probably not.

Failure is easy; success is demanding. For the Taste Buds, their corporate success might qualify them for suits, which is OK, as long as they are bathing suits. The beach is a long way, but not that long.

SEMOLINA'S BISTRO ITALIA
CRAWFISH ROBAN

The Taste Buds named this dish after Lionel Robin, a chef friend who serves up some of the best crawfish dishes in southeast Louisiana from Henderson, La., just east of Breaux Bridge. His name is pronounced Roban, but naming a crawfish dish after him was a challenge since no one would know how to say it correctly–hence the creative spelling of his name as it is said, not read.

SERVES: 6

ROBAN SAUCE

1/4 cup	unsalted butter
1/4 cup	garlic, minced
1 cup	green onions, finely chopped
1 quart	heavy whipping cream
1 tablespoon	blackened redfish seasoning (see page 92)
to taste	salt and white pepper

CRAWFISH ROBAN

1/4 cup	unsalted butter
1 pound	Louisiana crawfish tails, fresh or frozen
2 cups	Roban sauce
1 1/2 pounds	pasta shells, medium sized, cooked
1/4 cup	green onions, finely chopped

DIRECTIONS

Melt the butter in a 12-inch or larger heavy-bottomed saucepan. Add the garlic and green onions and cook over a medium fire until the garlic releases its flavor, about 3 minutes.

Pour in the heavy cream, reduce the heat, and cook over low heat. The sauce will be very thin until the mixture is reduced by nearly one-half. Stir the sauce often and do not allow the mixture to stick. The sauce is reduced to the proper consistency when it is thick enough to heavily coat the back of the spoon, about 20-30 minutes.

When the sauce is ready, add the blackened redfish seasoning and adjust with salt and pepper to taste.

Reduce the heat. Drain any liquid from the crawfish tails and add tails to the saucepan. Simmer over low heat, about 5 minutes.

Remove the sauce from the heat and pour over the cooked pasta. Toss to completely coat the pasta with the sauce. Taste and add salt and pepper as desired. Garnish with finely chopped green onions. Serve immediately.

Note: Louisiana shrimp may be used as a substitute for Louisiana crawfish. In fact, almost any combination of seafood with the Roban sauce and pasta is spectacular.

CRAWFISH THERMIDOR

An affable, creative man, Chef Frank stays busy cooking, teaching, and offering his many talents to help promote New Orleans cuisine. Any time is a good time to drive up River Road to Dante Street.

SERVES: 6 Appetizers

1/4 cup	French bread crumbs, fine	1 pinch	ground white pepper
2 tablespoons	Parmesan cheese, grated	1 pinch	ground cayenne pepper
2 tablespoons	unsalted butter, melted	1/2 cup	crawfish or seafood stock
1 tablespoon	ground paprika	2 cups	whipping cream
2 tablespoons	unsalted butter	2 tablespoons	Dijon mustard
1 cup	yellow onions, diced	2 tablespoons	unsalted butter
2 tablespoons	shallots, minced	1/2 cup	green onions,
1	bay leaf		thinly sliced
2 tablespoons	whole-leaf dried tarragon	1 pound	Louisiana crawfish tails,
1 teaspoon	salt		peeled

SEAFOOD STOCK

2 cups	shrimp, lobster, crawfish, or gumbo (small) crabs	2	bay leaves
1 large	onion, roughly chopped	1 sprig	fresh thyme
1 cup	celery, roughly chopped	1 head	garlic, cut in half
4 sprigs	parsley	5 whole	black peppercorns
1 medium	carrot, chopped	1/2 medium	lemon rind

DIRECTIONS

Prepare the crawfish or seafood stock. Place all ingredients in a large stockpot. Bring to a boil, reduce heat and simmer for 1 hour. Skim carefully. Remove from heat, strain, and set aside. In a mixing bowl, add the bread crumbs, Parmesan, melted butter, and paprika. Mix well and set aside.

To prepare the Thermidor sauce, melt 2 tablespoons of butter in a large skillet over medium-high heat. Add the onions, shallots, and bay leaf. Stirring occasionally, cook until the onions become soft and clear, 2-5 minutes. Add the tarragon, salt, white and cayenne peppers, and cook for 1 minute. Add the stock, and bring to a boil. Reduce the heat and simmer the stock over low heat, reduce the liquid by half. Raise the heat to medium-high heat, add the cream, Dijon mustard, and return to a boil. Reduce heat to low and simmer for 2-3 minutes. Remove from heat, strain, and set aside.

Melt the remaining 2 tablespoons butter in a large skillet over medium-high heat. Add the green onions and cook for 5 seconds. Add the crawfish and cook for 1 minute. Add the Thermidor sauce and bring to a boil. Spoon the Crawfish Thermidor into small baking dishes (or 1 larger casserole). Sprinkle the top of each dish with the bread crumb mixture. Place the ramekins under a broiler until the tops brown, 1-2 minutes. Carefully remove from the oven and allow to cool. Serve warm.

Named the James Beard Foundation's Best Chef Southeast in 1998 was a well-deserved accolade for Frank Brigtsen, the man many afficianados call one of new generation of New Orleans chefs who are working to revitalize Creole/Acadian cooking.

Co-owner of Brigtsen's with his wife Marna, he began his career as an apprentice under Chef Paul Prudhomme at Commander's Palace.

He followed Chef Paul to K-Paul's as night chef, then graduated to executive chef. In return, Paul and the late K Prudhomme were instrumental in helping Frank and Marna open their uptown restaurant in an old Victorian cottage at the curve of the river.

Gene Bourg, former restaurant critic for The Times-Picayune, described Frank's interpretation of Creole/Acadian food as a "reaffirmation that Louisiana cooking is America's most durable and satisfying. Brigtsen's is now the place against which all other restaurants serving South Louisiana cuisine have to be measured."

OYSTERS

In *A Moveable Feast*, Hemingway wrote, "As I ate the oysters with their strong taste of the sea and their faint metallic taste that the cold white wine washed away, leaving only the sea taste and the succulent texture, and as I drank their cold liquid from each shell and washed it down with the crisp taste of the wine, I lost the empty feeling and began to be happy and to make plans."

Standing at an oyster bar while the shucker keeps up with you is simple bliss. Oysters on the half shell – iridescent, shimmering in nature's little container.

In New Orleans it's not uncommon to buy a sack of fresh oysters for a festival at home, then eat a few raw while preparing the rest for a throw-down, a joyous gathering of family generations, friends, great food, great music in the backyard, a park, a fishing camp by a bayou, or on the lakefront. It does not matter where it is, nor does it make any difference whether it's called a throw-down or a fais do-do, everyone brings a dish and the host provides the main event.

New Orleans' P&J Oyster Company has been in the bivalve business since 1876, first cultivating, harvesting, and distributing them. Today, P&J is the country's longest continuously operating shucking house. They supply fresh Gulf oysters to the finest restaurants. They will also provide oysters to enthusiastic individuals. Simply ask.

You should be warned that it takes a crowd to eat a sack of oysters, but if word gets out, a crowd will gather and be waiting wherever you say. Not one of them will remember or care that Jonathan Swift in *Polite Conversations* about 250 years ago observed, "He was a bold man that first eat an oyster."

No, he was probably just hungry.

A raffish French Quarter hole-in-the-wall, Acme also serves other seafood, but prepare to make new friends at the oyster bar as you watch your dozen or more opened, or sit at a table and order a feast of raw, boiled, broiled, and fried seafood.

Acme is best known for raw oysters on the half shell but that isn't a recipe. Open the oyster, dip it in cocktail sauce, or not, and that's all there is to eating one. Their broiled oysters are but one variation on the grilled/broiled theme.

Open since 1910, the Acme Oyster House® is a New Orleans seafood institution.

ACME OYSTER HOUSE®
GRILLED OYSTERS

Grilled oysters have been around about as long as the barbecue pit, but several New Orleans restaurants have made them a mystical experience. Since nature brings us the oyster already ensconced in its own pan-shaped shell, all that is required to grill it is to open it, discard the top shell and cut the muscle attaching the oyster to the bottom shell.

SERVES: 4

1 pound	salted butter	1 tablespoon	Worcestershire sauce
2 bunches	green onions, finely chopped	2 tablespoons	Creole seasonings (page 92)
20 toes	fresh garlic, puree	1/4 cup	dry white wine
1 teaspoon	crushed red pepper	2 dozen	oysters, freshly shucked, on the half shell
3 tablespoons	fresh thyme, finely chopped		
3 tablespoons	fresh oregano, finely chopped	1 cup	Romano cheese, grated
2 tablespoons	fresh lemon juice	1 loaf	French bread

DIRECTIONS

The butter garlic sauce should be prepared just prior to grilling the oysters. In a large sauté pan add 1/2 pound of butter and place over a medium heat. Add green onions, garlic, red pepper, thyme, oregano, lemon juice, Worcestershire sauce, and Creole seasonings. Cook for 2 minutes, and add the white wine.

Stir ingredients continuously and cook until green onions are soft. Remove the garlic sauce from the heat and allow to cool for 3 minutes.

In a large mixing bowl, add the remaining butter and garlic sauce. Blend until the butter is folded into the sauce. The resulting butter garlic sauce should have a creamy consistency.

Preheat the grill to 350°F.

Place the freshly shucked oysters on the half shell in the center of the grill. Once the water around the oyster begins to bubble and the oyster begins to rise, ladle 1 tablespoon of the butter garlic sauce on top of each oyster. (*Note: Make sure that the sauce is well blended.*) This ensures the proper blend of butter and seasonings.

Top with 1/2 tablespoon of grated Romano cheese. Allow the cheese to melt. Oysters should brown slightly around the edges. Remove oysters and place on a heat-resistant plate or platter. While still hot add another tablespoon of butter sauce to the top of each oyster.

Serve immediately with warm French bread for dipping.

ARNAUD'S
OYSTERS BIENVILLE

Arnaud's original Oysters Bienville takes its name from the restaurant's location at 813 rue Bienville, which in turn was named for the founder of New Orleans, Jean Baptiste le Moyne, Sieur de Bienville, governor of the original French Colony. As the story goes, the Count created Oysters Bienville as a competitive response to the great attention Oysters Rockefeller was attracting at Antoine's, so named because of the richness of the recipe.

SERVES: 4

1 tablespoon	vegetable oil	1/4 cup	dry bread crumbs
2/3 cup	white mushrooms, finely chopped	1/4 cup	flat-leaf parsley, finely chopped
4 tablespoons	unsalted butter	1/4 teaspoon	cayenne pepper
1 1/2 teaspoons	garlic, very finely chopped	1 teaspoon	kosher or sea salt
4 large	shallots, finely chopped	to taste	freshly ground black pepper
1/2 pound	cooked shrimp, finely chopped	2 dozen	plump, salty, freshly shucked oysters, flat sides of the shells reserved
1 tablespoon	all-purpose flour		
1/2 cup	brandy	2 pounds	rock salt, optional
1/2 cup	heavy cream	for serving	lemon wedges
6 tablespoons	grated Romano cheese		

DIRECTIONS

In a large heavy saucepan, heat the oil and sauté the mushrooms for 4 minutes. Remove from the pan with a slotted spoon, discard the liquid.

In the same pan, melt the butter over low heat and sauté the garlic and shallots for about 3 minutes, stirring frequently, until softened. Add the diced shrimp and stir to mix, then sprinkle evenly with the flour. Stir together, add the reserved mushrooms and increase the heat to medium.

Stirring constantly, deglaze the pan with brandy. Stir in the cream and cook for 2-3 minutes, until smooth. Stir in the Romano, dry bread crumbs, parsley, cayenne, salt, and black pepper to taste. The mixture should be a soft, moundable consistency. A small amount of milk may be added if the mixture is too thick. Remove the pan from the heat and transfer mixture to a glass bowl. Cool the Bienville mixture to room temperature, then refrigerate for about 1-2 hours, or until thoroughly chilled.

Preheat the oven to 400°F. Wash the oyster shells well, and pat dry. Drain the oysters and place 1 in each of the 24 shells, or use 2 smaller oysters per shell if necessary. Place the shells in a large, heavy roasting pan lined with a 1/2-inch layer of rock salt, or place 6 filled oyster shells in each of 4 pie pans lined with salt (the salt keeps the shells upright during cooking). Top each oyster with 1 generous tablespoon of the Bienville mix and bake for 15 to 18 minutes, or until nicely browned.

The shells will be extremely hot. Carefully place 6 oysters on each hot dinner plate. If baked in pie pans of rock salt, place each pan on a dinner plate. Garnish with a lemon wedge and serve.

The grande dame of French Quarter restaurants, Arnaud's encompasses thirteen historic buildings. It has been family owned and operated since 1918 when Count Arnaud Cazenave founded it. Archie and Jane Casbarian acquired the establishment in 1978 and set about a top to bottom refurbishment.

A glittering beveled glass wall sparkles the main dining room with crystal chandeliers and ceiling fans over the original Italian mosaic floors. Each mosaic pattern changes from building to building.

Oysters Bienville was created here, only one of many dishes that trace their origins to the historic establishment.

Today, the entire Casbarian family continues to hold Arnaud's close. They have added Remoulade, an oyster bar for the casual side of Creole cooking next door, and greatly expanded private dining for both restaurants. The new Jazz Bistro offers Arnaud's menu to the accompaniment of live Dixieland jazz music with dinner.

Archie and Jane Casbarian have brought the next generation into management, their son Archie, and daughter Katy. It's all in the family. Always has been. Always will be.

As Arnaud's maintains its secret rémoulade recipe, Antoine's keeps the Oysters Rockefeller's recipe a secret as well. Antoine's insists that there is no spinach in that recipe, but it has not stopped restaurants around the world from producing fairly accurate versions of it with spinach.

Arnaud's Chef Tommy DiGiovanni does use spinach as one of the greens in his interpretation. No self-respecting New Orleans seafood book would be complete without an Oysters Rockefeller recipe, so this one comes compliments of Chef Tommy as the dish is served at Arnaud's. Tommy has cooked for celebrities, heads of state, royalty, and presidents. Not one of them has left unsatisfied.

Oysters Rockefeller is also an excellent hors d'oeuvres, minus the shell and served in a little pastry cup. I've also seen Oysters Rockefeller soup, flan, and even pizza. The flavors lend themselves to almost any treatment.

"How ya like dem ersters?" asked New Orleans' Mayor Robert Maestri at Antoine's as he and President Franklin Roosevelt dined on Oysters Rockefeller.

We offer thanks, and a tip of the toque to Antoine's.

CHEF GAETANO DIGIOVANNI
OYSTERS ROCKEFELLER

Antoine's, as the oldest family-owned restaurant in America, is famous for its creation of Oysters Rockefeller, which proved that baked oysters are wonderful, especially if the topping is extraordinary. That auspicious start has given inspiration to chefs around the world, who can and will do almost anything to present an oyster.

SERVES: 6

2 tablespoons	unsalted butter	1 pinch	dried thyme
12 slices	raw bacon, very finely chopped	1 pinch	cayenne pepper
4 cups	celery, finely chopped	2 tablespoons	flat leaf parsley, finely chopped
1 cup	green bell pepper, finely chopped	1/3 cup	Herbsaint® liqueur or Pernod
3 tablespoons	garlic, very finely chopped	1 tablespoon	fresh basil, finely chopped
1 cup	white onions, finely chopped	to taste	kosher or sea salt
4 cups	spinach, blanched, drained and chopped	to taste	freshly ground black pepper
2	bay leaves	3 dozen	salty oysters, freshly shucked, flat sides of shells reserved
		2 pounds	rock salt (optional)
		for garnish	lemon wedges

DIRECTIONS

In a medium sauté pan, melt the butter over medium heat and cook the bacon until the fat has been rendered and bacon is crisp, about 5 minutes.

Add the celery, green pepper, garlic, and onions, then sauté until the vegetables are softened, 4 to 5 minutes. Add the spinach and stir for 5 more minutes. Stir in the bay leaves and thyme, cayenne, and parsley, then drizzle in the Herbsaint, and continue cooking for 1 minute. Reduce heat and simmer for 2 more minutes. Remove the bay leaves, add the basil and season to taste with salt and pepper.

In a blender or food processor, purée the mixture in batches if necessary. Place the purée back into the original pan, mixing thoroughly. Transfer to a covered container, cool to room temperature and refrigerate for about 1 hour or until the mixture is firm.

Preheat the oven to 400°F.

Wash the flat oyster shells well, and pat them dry. Drain the oysters and place one in each prepared shell. Place the shells in a large, heavy roasting pan lined with 1/2-inch layer of rock salt, or place 6 oyster shells in each of 6 pie pans lined with salt (the salt keeps the shells upright during cooking and stops the delicious juices from escaping). Top each oyster with 1 generous tablespoon of Rockefeller sauce and bake for 15 to 18 minutes, until nicely browned.

The shells will be extremely hot. Carefully place 6 oysters on each warm dinner plate. If baked in pie pans of rock salt, place each pan on a dinner plate. The salt retains the heat and should not be eaten.

Garnish with a lemon wedge and serve immediately.

UGLESICH'S
OYSTER SHOOTERS

Served in a cocktail glass or on the half shell, oyster shooters are the perfect first course or cocktail party hors d'oeuvre. Knock one back; reach for another. Gail Uglesich prepared these on Martha Stewart Living's weekday television show. We have provided two other recipes so you can get into the hot and cold spirit of creativity. The shooter on the lower left is from Uglesich's.

SERVES: 6

2 cups	olive oil (not extra-virgin)	1/2 teaspoon	dried thyme
1/2 cup	balsamic vinegar	1/2 teaspoon	dried oregano
1/4 cup	Steen's® cane syrup	2 tablespoons	sun-dried tomatoes, minced
1 teaspoon	salt		(dried, not packed in oil)
1 teaspoon	ground black pepper	24 large	freshly shucked oysters, in
1 teaspoon	cayenne pepper		their own liquor
1/2 teaspoon	dried basil		

Shuck the oysters, reserving the shells. Mix all the ingredients except the oysters, and let the marinade sit. The longer it sits, the better it gets.

Sauté oysters over medium heat in 4 batches in a 1/2 cup of the marinade for each batch, until the edges just begin to curl. Do not overcook! Place each oyster back in a shell. Drizzle a small amount of hot marinade from the pan onto each oyster. Keep warm until all batches are done.

Serve 4 oysters per person, on the half shell, or in small cocktail glasses.

Note: The extra sauce can be refrigerated and used again. One particular customer liked to use the sauce over his fried soft shell crab. Recipe courtesy of Uglesich's Restaurant Cookbook.

MIGNONETTE SAUCE

1 cup	red wine vinegar
1/2 cup	shallots, finely chopped
1/2 teaspoon	coarsely ground black pepper
dash	kosher salt

In a small bowl, mix all ingredients together and chill.

COCKTAIL SAUCE

1 cup	ketchup
1/4 cup	prepared horseradish
1 tablespoon	fresh lemon juice
1 teaspoon	Worcestershire sauce
dash	Tabasco™ sauce

In a small bowl, mix all ingredients together and chill.

Patrons had lined the block the day Uglesich's closed in 2007 for a final, memorable taste. It got hungry out the next day, and the days after. No lines of diners waiting in the sun. Located on Baronne Street it was a straight shot from the federal and state courthouses and office buildings.

The menu was a myriad of seafood specialties from simple to simply out of this world. There was no pretense, no posturing. Wait your turn. No reservations were accepted for the inside ten tables. They were supplemented with six outside tables several years later.

Judges sat next to felons, lawyers next to laborers inside the packed dining room, at the bar, or outside at rickety wooden tables and chairs. It was democracy in action spurred on by the common need of fresh seafood, served hot or cold, to order, right now.

Sam Uglesich started the restaurant in the 1920s, never moved, and never expanded. Sam's son Tony and Tony's wife Miss Gail, as she was known to the customers, took it from a fried seafood place to a restaurant offering appetizers and specialty dishes. Dessert was not offered.

In 1919 Joe Casamento opened his restaurant, which is still run by members of the family in the finest New Orleans tradition by Joe Casamento's son, Joseph and grandson/nephew, CJ with his wife, Linda Gerdes.

They operate the kind of restaurant everyone would like to have. Their products feature fresh seafood, especially oysters, and the only frustration is when the Magazine Street establishment has the "closed" sign on the front door.

They take off during June, July, August and all major holidays. Somehow that is usually when I've got a hankering for an oyster loaf or a bowl of soup.

Casamento's bakes its own pan bread, especially luscious when stuffed with shrimp or oysters.

Notably, when the restaurant was built, Joe Casemento felt that tile would be easier to keep sparkling clean. Consequently, the restaurant's walls and floors are a panorama of mosaic tile, sparkling clean.

CASAMENTO'S
OYSTER SOUP

SERVES: 4-6

3 1/2 cups	water		1/8 teaspoon	thyme, dried
2 dozen	freshly shucked oysters, drained		1/8 teaspoon	red pepper, ground
1/2 cup	celery, chopped		1	bay leaf
1/2 cup	green onions, chopped		3/4 cup	heavy whipping cream
1/2 cup	onions, chopped		2 cups	whole milk
1/4 cup	unsalted butter		1/2 cup	all-purpose flour
1/2 teaspoon	garlic, finely chopped		1 teaspoon	kosher or sea salt
			1/4 teaspoon	ground white pepper

DIRECTIONS

In a medium saucepan bring the water to boil. Add the oysters and cook for 3 minutes. Remove oysters with a slotted spoon and reserve 3 cups of liquid. Set both aside.

In a Dutch oven over medium heat cook celery, green onions, and onions in 1 tablespoon of butter, stirring constantly until tender. Stir in 2 1/2 cups of the reserved liquid, garlic, thyme, red pepper, and bay leaf; bring to a boil. Stir in the cream, reduce the heat and simmer for 5 minutes. Stir in the milk and return to a simmer.

Melt the remaining butter in a small saucepan over low heat. Add the flour, stirring until smooth. Cook 1 minute, stirring constantly, then cook for about 3 more minutes until smooth (the mixture will be very thick).

Gradually add the flour mixture to the saucepan, stirring with a wire whisk until blended. Add oysters, salt, and white pepper. Cook until thoroughly heated. Remove from the heat, discard bay leaf and serve immediately.

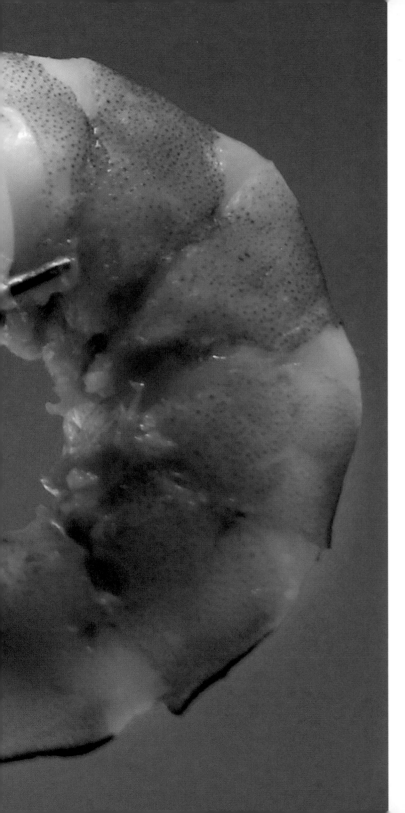

SHRIMP

Shrimp takes the spotlight in New Orleans.

An out-of-town restaurant group opened here with an appetizer of shrimp in cocktail sauce for $2 each. It took no time for bets to get laid on how long that restaurant would last. Not long. We serve shrimp by the pound, not the piece. What would you do with one shrimp? Would it be legal?

Shrimp are versatile and abundant. They are easy to peel and easier to serve in the shell in a seasoned boil, a sauce, fried, or sautéd. Shrimp make wonderful appearances in jambalaya, gumbo, stew, over pasta, or on the grill.

If you like to experiment with seafood, shrimp is your friend. Hot or cold.

To help you figure out servings, seafood is sold by the pound and the count. A pound of jumbo shrimp contains 16 to 25, large 26 to 35, medium 36 to 50, and unless there is some special reason, you don't want to bother with anything smaller.

Unless they are river shrimp.

Tiny river shrimp are hard to find and are a rare treat. They are not often available and sell for a premium, especially if they are peeled, for the obvious reason.

When buying head-on, in-shell shrimp, about 1/3 the weight is heads and shells, but while this is debris, it is not waste. Save the heads and shells to make a shrimp stock for future use in soups, stews, and sauces. Freeze the peelings in zip lock bags until there is enough to make a stock. The recipe for any seafood stock is on page 61. Once made, the stock also freezes beautifully.

It's hard to find something that shrimp does not do well. They are multi-talented on the culinary arts stage.

Chef Emeril Lagasse has made New Orleans his own, using creativity, a sense of humor and a big heart. Here, he takes a traditional dish and gives it a twist by adding cream and his own seasonings. He, too, has been named a Best Chef Southeast by the James Beard Society.

EMERIL's CREOLE SEASONING™

YIELD: 3/4 CUP

3 tablespoons	paprika
2 tablespoons	salt
2 teaspoons	garlic powder
1 teaspoon	black pepper
1 tablespoon	onion powder
1 teaspoon	cayenne pepper
1 teaspoon	dried oregano
1 teaspoon	dried thyme
1/2 teaspoon	celery salt

ROSEMARY BISCUITS

YIELD: 12 BISCUITS

1 cup	all-purpose flour
1 teaspoon	baking powder
1/8 teaspoon	baking soda
1/2 teaspoon	salt
3 tablespoons	unsalted butter, diced and chilled
1 tablespoon	fresh rosemary, minced
1/2 cup	buttermilk, or as needed

Recipe with permission from *Essence of Emeril*

EMERIL'S
BARBECUED SHRIMP WITH ROSEMARY BISCUITS

SERVES: 4

BARBECUED SHRIMP

2 pounds	shrimp, in their shells		2 cups	water
2 tablespoons	Emeril's Creole Seasoning™		1/2 cup	Worcestershire sauce
1 tablespoon	ground black pepper		1/4 cup	dry white wine
2 tablespoons	olive oil		1/4 teaspoon	salt
1/4 cup	onions, chopped		2 cups	heavy cream
2 tablespoons	garlic, minced		2 tablespoons	butter
3	bay leaves		1 tablespoon	chopped chives
3	lemons, peeled and sectioned			

DIRECTIONS

Peel the shrimp, leaving the tails intact. Reserve the shells and set aside. In a large mixing bowl, toss shrimp with 1/2 tablespoon black pepper and 1 tablespoon of the Emeril's Creole Seasoning™. Be sure to coat them well. Refrigerate the shrimp while you make the sauce.

Heat 1 tablespoon of oil in a 12-inch skillet over high heat. When oil is hot, add the onions and garlic. Sauté for 1 minute. Add the reserved shrimp shells, the remaining Creole seasoning, bay leaves, lemons, water, Worcestershire, wine, salt, and remaining black pepper. Stir well and bring to a boil. Reduce the heat and simmer for 30 minutes. Remove from the heat, allow to cool for about 15 minutes. Strain into a small saucepan. Place over high heat, bring to a boil, and cook until thick, syrupy, and dark brown, about 15 minutes. Makes about 4-5 tablespoons of barbecue sauce base.

Heat the remaining olive oil in a large skillet over high heat. When the oil is hot, add the seasoned shrimp and sauté them, occasionally shaking the skillet, for 2 minutes. Add the cream and all of the barbecue base. Stir and simmer for 3 minutes. Transfer the shrimp to a warm platter with tongs or a slotted spoon. Whisk in the butter, when fully incorporated, remove from heat. Mound the shrimp in the center of a platter. Spoon the sauce over the shrimp and around the plate. Arrange the biscuits around the shrimp. Garnish with chopped chives. Serve with petite rosemary biscuits.

ROSEMARY BISCUITS

Preheat the oven to 425°F.

Sift the flour, baking powder, baking soda, and salt into a mixing bowl. Cut the butter into the flour with a pastry blender or a fork, or rub between your fingers, until the mixture resembles coarse crumbs. Stir in the rosemary. Stir in the 1/2 cup buttermilk a few tablespoons at a time. Knead the dough in the bowl just until it holds together, adding additional buttermilk, a tablespoon at a time, if the dough is too dry. Take care not to overwork the dough, or the biscuits will be tough rather than light and airy. On a lightly floured surface, pat the dough into a circle about 7 inches in diameter and 1/2 inch thick. Using a 1-inch round cookie cutter, cut out 12 biscuits. Place the biscuits on a large baking sheet. Bake until golden on top and lightly browned on the bottom, about 12 minutes.

UPPERLINE
FRIED GREEN TOMATOES
WITH SHRIMP RÉMOULADE

SERVES: 4 Appetizers

RÉMOULADE SAUCE

1/2 cup	Creole mustard		to taste	salt
2 tablespoons	ketchup		1/2 cup	olive oil
1 teaspoon	Worcestershire sauce		1/4 cup	heart of celery, finely chopped
2 teaspoons	prepared horseradish		1 1/2 teaspoon	parsley, finely chopped
1 teaspoon	garlic, finely chopped		1 tablespoon	white or yellow onions, grated
1 teaspoon	fresh lemon juice		1 tablespoon	green onions tops, finely chopped
1 1/2 teaspoon	paprika		to taste	Tabasco™ sauce
1/8 teaspoon	ground white pepper			
1/8 teaspoon	cayenne pepper			

DIRECTIONS

Combine the Creole mustard, ketchup, Worcestershire, horseradish, garlic, lemon juice, paprika, white pepper, cayenne pepper, and salt to taste. Mix well. Place the mixture in a blender on low speed and add the olive oil in a slow stream.

Add the celery, parsley, onions, green onions, and mix well. Add Tabasco™ sauce to taste. The sauce should be spicy and tangy. If the sauce is too spicy, add a little more oil. If the sauce is too tangy, add a pinch or two of sugar. Cover and chill before use. If covered and refrigerated, the sauce should keep for several days.

FRIED GREEN TOMATOES

1 cup	buttermilk		5 tablespoons	vegetable oil or very light olive oil
8 slices	green tomatoes, (completely green if possible), 1/2-inch thick		handful	mixed greens
1 cup	corn flour*, lightly seasoned with salt and black pepper		24 medium	shrimp, poached, peeled and chilled
			1 cup	rémoulade sauce

DIRECTIONS

Heat oil in a 12-inch or larger sauté pan over medium heat. Meanwhile, dip tomato slices in the buttermilk, then coat with corn flour*. Carefully place tomato slices in sauté pan and cook slowly, until golden brown on the bottom. Do not move the tomatoes until ready to turn them over. Carefully flip the slices to brown other side. (*Note: If cooked too fast, the inside does not get cooked before the outside browns.*)

The tomatoes are served warm or hot. The shrimp and rémoulade sauce should be cold. On individual serving plates, place 2 slices of warm tomatoes next to each other on a bed of mixed greens. Top each slice with 3 or 4 chilled, cooked shrimp, then top with 1-2 tablespoons of rémoulade sauce.

*or finely ground corn meal

As the owner, JoAnn Clevenger has made the Upperline her home, and she is the welcoming hostess. She is fond of saying that "New Orleans is extraordinarily beautiful. Look at the music we have, the architecture, the flowers. We're very lucky. And you know, it's not just where you're going, but the in between part – how you get there – that matters."

Dining at the Upperline is one of the ways to get there. Although the dish is common in New Orleans today, the original fried green tomato with shrimp rémoulade combination was created at the Upperline in 1992.

Executive Chef Ken Smith has commanded the kitchen for almost a decade, following Chef Tom Cowman.

Dr. Rise Ochsner immortalized Chef Tom with a magnificent portrait, which hangs in the art-filled dining room. It is a grand and quirky collection, not unlike the combination of classic and contemporary cuisine that is modern New Orleans. Tom Cowman and Ken Smith, in their own ways, contributed to both.

Wayne Baquet is the last active restaurateur from New Orleans first family of Creole soul. He's the son of the well-known culinary family that has operated 12 different restaurants, and he carries on the tradition with panache.

The family's first restaurant was named Chicken Coop 60 years ago, then came Eddie's, where a cigar box was the cash register and the whole family lived in the back. Eddie's was a favorite of Bill Cosby, who talked about it on "The Tonight Show." Other restaurants followed, ending with Zachery's, which the family sold.

Li'l Dizzy's on Esplanade Avenue joins the long parade of Baquet restaurants. Although it serves only breakfast and lunch, its fans crowd the place twice a day looking for a little "Creole Soul".

Wayne Baquet is a gracious man who enjoys pleasing the crowds he attracts, and is himself as happy with white beans and rice as he would be with a grander meal.

LI'L DIZZY'S CAFE
SHRIMP CREOLE

The Baquet family has been called the Creole Kings. Wayne Sr. pointed out that while you would never find chitterlings in a Wayne Baquet restaurant, the food served is soul, but Creole soul. "Creole food is crawfish bisque, crawfish pie, red beans, jambalaya, gumbo." In an article in the *Times-Picayune* he said, "Creole food in New Orleans is cooked by people in New Orleans who are Creole." See how simple it is when someone who understands explains it?

SERVES: 4

1 cup	vegetable oil	3	fresh bay leaves, crushed
3/4 cup	all-purpose flour	2 1/2 cups	water
1 1/2 medium	onions, finely chopped	1/4 teaspoon	fresh oregano, chopped
5 toes	garlic, whole	1/2 large	fresh lemon, juiced
2 bunches	green onions (green part finely chopped, white part roughly chopped)	1/4 teaspoon	cayenne pepper
		to taste	salt
1/2 large	green bell pepper, finely chopped	2 1/2 pounds	shrimp, peeled and deveined
1 1/2 cans	tomato sauce (12 ounces)	2 cups	Uncle Ben's® converted or long grain white rice
1 teaspoon	fresh thyme, chopped		

DIRECTIONS

Begin by preparing the rice. In a 6-8 quart pot, put 4 quarts of cold water and a teaspoon of salt. When the water comes to a rapid boil, add the rice. Boil uncovered over high heat 15-20 minutes or until tender. Test frequently after 15 minutes of cooking time. When the rice is tender, drain in a colander and rinse with cold water. Leave the rice in the colander and set aside until ready to serve.

Prepare the Creole sauce. Plan the time carefully, once the roux has been started, it must attended and constantly stirred. Heat the oil in a large heavy-bottomed saucepan. Gradually add the flour, a little at a time, stirring constantly. Cook over medium to low heat until a medium brown roux (the color of peanut butter) is formed, about 20-30 minutes. Remove from heat and add the onions, garlic, green onions, and bell peppers. Mix well, then return to low heat and cook, stirring constantly, until the vegetables become soft and translucent, about 4-6 minutes.

Add in the tomato sauce, thyme, bay leaves, oregano, and lemon juice. Return the heat to medium high and bring to a low boil. Add the water and mix thoroughly. When the mixture comes to a boil again, reduce the heat. Add cayenne pepper and salt to taste. Allow the sauce to simmer, about 30-45 minutes.

Add the shrimp and allow to come to a low boil, then cover. Reduce the heat slightly and simmer for 20 minutes. Remove the pot from the heat and allow to stand, covered for about 10 minutes before serving. Steam the rice, over a small pot of water for 5 minutes, to reheat it.

Garnish with fresh parsley sprigs if desired.

CHEF JOHN FOLSE
SHRIMP MOUSSE

A superb appetizer, canape, hors d'oeuvre or entrée, Shrimp Mousse can be presented as a mold, fill halved, hollowed bell peppers or tomatoes and a guaranteed hit when presented in its colorful flavors. In fact, there is no reason why crawfish or crabmeat could not be substituted for the shrimp to make one recipe work as three different variations.

SERVES: 20

3 cups	boiled shrimp, chopped		1 tablespoon	fresh lemon juice
4	catfish fillets, poached		1 tablespoon	cooking sherry
1 cup	mayonnaise		1 tablespoon	Worcestershire sauce
1/2 cup	sour cream		1/2 teaspoon	Louisiana hot sauce
1 tablespoon	minced garlic		2 packages	unflavored gelatin
1/4 cup	parsley, finely chopped		1/2 teaspoon	salt
1/4 cup	red bell peppers, finely chopped		1 teaspoon	black pepper
1/4 cup	yellow bell peppers, finely chopped			

DIRECTIONS

The shrimp are boiled in a seafood boil mixture and will cook quickly. They will turn pink and firm in about 3-5 minutes. You may purchase a crab and seafood boil seasonings liquid and follow the package directions or use the recipe (see page 54). Allow the shrimp to cool, chop and refrigerate.

This poaching recipe can be found (see page 87). Pour the poaching liquid into a large saucepan. Heat the liquid until it comes to a slight boil, place fish fillets in the pan. The poaching liquid should cover the fillets. Lower the heat and poach the fish for 7-10 minutes. Remove the fish from the pan, strain and reserve the liquid.

Sprinkle the gelatin over 1 cup of cold poaching liquid in a bowl, let stand for 1 minute until gelatin has dissolved. In a small saucepan heat the gelatin mixture until completely incorporated.

Coarsely chop the poached fish and place in a large mixing bowl. When the gelatin has completely dissolved, add all of the remaining ingredients for the mousse. Thoroughly blend all ingredients together. Taste, and adjust seasonings as desired.

Pour mixture into a mold, tap the mold on the table to settle the mixture evenly and to remove excess air. Cover with plastic wrap and refrigerate overnight.

Remove the mousse from the mold. Using a wet paring knife loosen the edges of the mold. Place a warm cloth on the top to release. Remove the cloth and place a serving platter on top of the mold and carefully flip the mousse onto the platter.

Serve sliced with French bread, on top of small toasted slices of baguettes, with crackers for appetizers or fill colorful bell pepper halves.

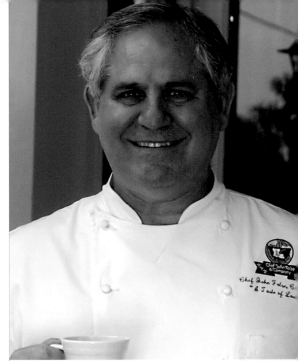

To say John Folse is simply a chef is called burying the lead. He honors and shares his profession through the Chef John Folse Culinary Institute at Nicholls State University.

Lafitte's Landing Restaurant at Bittersweet Plantation in historic downtown Donaldsonville is his showcase for a B&B and dinner guests.

Chef Folse's seventh book is The Encyclopedia of Cajun and Creole Cuisine, *an authoritative collection of Louisiana's culture and cuisine. He runs a major food distributorship and manufactures his own product line.*

That's when he's not traveling the world to promote Louisiana and Creole cuisine. In his spare time, Folse is a frequent guest on radio and television programs, including his own.

He quietly gives back, supporting other chefs. When Leah Chase was asked to entertain President George W. Bush's party in her completed, yet unopened restaurant, Folse's truck pulled up with staff, equipment, food and everything necessary to make New Orleans proud.

Antoine's, Madame Begue's, and Tujaque's were the first eateries in a city that is now known for its elegant, even exotic, sometime expensive dining. It's good to remember that it did not start that way. It started because working stiffs had to get some food in them to keep working.

That was even more obvious when Madame Hippolyte Begue opened the city's second restaurant in 1853 at the corner of Decatur and Madison. To meet the needs of dockworkers and French Market laborers she served an elaborate, multi-course breakfast at 11 a.m. Was it the first brunch in the country? Could be.

Tujaque's Restaurant opened in 1856 and moved to Madame Begue's premises when she closed, so two of the first three restaurants in the city were at the same location, which can be a little confusing. What is clear, however, is that Tujaque's still serves a fine example of the classic Creole meal of boiled beef and an especially tangy red remoulade sauce over boiled shrimp on a bed of chopped lettuce.

Antoine's was the first restaurant in New Orleans because it was "an establishment that served food to the public." It was actually a boarding house that sold meals. When it opened in 1840, there wasn't any need for an up-scale restaurant. The Civil War was in the future, and domestic slaves made dining and entertaining at home easy and convenient for the owners, so that's what the wealthy upper class did. Only the working class ate out.

TUJAQUE'S
SHRIMP RÉMOULADE

If it is an original you are seeking, it would be Tujaque's on Decatur Street at the edge of the French Quarter, beside the French Market where its original guests worked. When we asked about the finely chopped lettuce incorporated into the rémoulade sauce, we were told it had been added to extend the sauce ages ago during hard times, and the recipe has never changed.

SERVES:

REMOULADE SAUCE	
1-1/2 cups	white onions, chopped finely
1 cup	celery, chopped finely
1/2 cup	green onions, chopped finely
1/2 cup	parsely, chopped finely
1/2 cup	iceberg lettuce, chopped finely
8 ounces	Creole or brown mustard
1 cup	olive oil
	paprika, generous amount, for color
1 ounce	fresh lemon juice
shredded	iceberg lettuce, for serving

BOILED SHRIMP	
2 pounds	shrimp, 15-20 count size, boiled
1 quart	water
1 tablespoon	cayenne or red pepper
1	bay leaf
20	black peppercorns
3 sprigs	thyme (or 1 teaspoon dry thyme)
1 teaspoon	marjoram
3 cloves	garlic
1 medium	onion, quartered
1 large	lemon, quartered salt to taste

DIRECTIONS

BOILED SHRIMP
Boil the shrimp with the heads and shells on to capture the seasonings. In a medium saucepan, bring 1 quart of water to a boil. Add the cayenne pepper, bay leaf, peppercorns, thyme, marjoram, garlic, onions, lemon and salt and pepper to taste. Allow the mixture to come to a full boil. Add the shrimp, with head and shells, to the boiling mixture. Allow the shrimp to boil for 3-5 minutes, and then remove from heat. Let the shrimp sit in the seafood boil mixture for 10-15 minutes so they absorb the seasonings. Drain the water, peel, and devein the shrimp. Allow the shrimp to chill in the refrigerator.

RÉMOULADE SAUCE
In a medium-sized mixing bowl combine the white onions, celery, green onions, parsley and chopped lettuce. Add the Creole mustard or brown mustard and mix well. Place all ingredients into a food processor or blender, chop briefly. Slowly add the olive oil while blending. Add salt and black pepper to taste.

The sauce should be a reddish brown color. Slowly add the paprika and stir until the sauce becomes the desired color. If the sauce is a little tangy, add a pinch of sugar to stabilize the taste. Chill in the refrigerator. The sauce can be made in advance and will keep for several days.

To serve, remove cooked shrimp and sauce from the refrigerator. Arrange five or six shrimp on a bed of shredded iceberg lettuce, on a saucer or cocktail glass. Pour the chilled rémoulade sauce over the shrimp. Serve cold.

DOOKY CHASE'S
STEWED SHRIMP

Stewed shrimp is one of those dishes not often seen outside of private kitchens. It's an old-fashioned Creole favorite, also known as shrimps and rice.

SERVES: 4

1/4 cup	vegetable oil
2 tablespoons	all-purpose flour
1/2 cup	onions, chopped
1/2 cup	celery, chopped
2 cloves	garlic, mashed and chopped
2 cans	tomato sauce (16 ounces)
2 cups	water
1/2 cup	green bell pepper, seeded and diced
1 tablespoon	Lawry's®seasoned salt
1 teaspoon	red pepper flakes
1 teaspoon	dried thyme leaves
2 tablespoons	parsley, chopped
2 large	white potatoes, peeled and quartered
1 pound	shrimp, peeled and deveined
4 cups	cooked long grain rice

DIRECTIONS

In a heavy-bottomed 6- to 8-quart pot or deep cast-iron skillet, heat the oil over medium heat. When the oil is hot, gradually stir in the flour. Cook over a low heat, stirring constantly, using a wooden spoon. Cook the flour until it forms a medium brown roux, about 20-30 minutes. The roux will be very hot, use caution while stirring. Do not allow the roux to stick to the bottom of the pot. If the roux sticks or burns, discard the mixture and start over. A roux that sticks or burns will give the finished dish a bitter and scorched taste.

When the roux is the color of peanut butter, lower the heat, and add the chopped onions and celery. Sauté the vegetables until the onions are translucent, about 7-10 minutes. Add the garlic, tomato sauce, and simmer for 10 more minutes.

Slowly add the water, stirring as you pour. Be careful not to leave lumps. Continue to stir, add bell pepper, seasoned salt, pepper, thyme, parsley. Increase the heat to medium and allow to come to a boil. Cook for 5 minutes.

Add potatoes and continue cooking for 10 minutes. Lower the fire and add the cleaned shrimp. Let the stew simmer until the potatoes and shrimp are done, about 10 minutes.

Serve over cooked white rice and garnish with parsley.

Her smile is as wide and welcoming as her heart. Chef Leah Chase, lovingly known as the "Queen of Creole Cuisine," at an energetic 85, represents the roots of what we do. She made good use of the same stove for 50 years, cooking for such luminaries as the Rev. Martin Luther King, Jr., Duke Ellington, Thurgood Marshall, James Baldwin, and Ray Charles. Now, she has a new stove and even more memories.

Before desegregation, it was a place for people of color. Today, race, creed or zip code doesn't matter a whit at Dooky Chase's. Leah and her husband Dooky created one of the country's most culturally significant restaurants.

Following Hurricane Katrina, the restaurant faced a tough two-year comeback. Leah and Dooky have given so much that asking for help never occurred to them. Bit by bit they started rebuilding and refurbishing.

It was time for others to return the favor. Spontaneous support, gifts and contributions—large and small—arrived from friends, restaurateurs, patrons, and colleagues.

Chef Leah says that one should strive to make a person feel his or her worth, that this is a true measure of a person. "I had to get back on my feet," she told me, "so I can start giving back." Leah, you never stopped.

Chef Austin Leslie inspired an offbeat CBS sitcom in 1987-88 based on his restaurant, Chez Hélène. His sideburns and captain's hat added personal flavor to "Frank's Place."

African-American neighborhoods celebrated restaurants such as Chez Hélène, Dooky Chase's, and Eddie's. Chef Leslie elevated Creole cooking through French and African influences creating a number of signature recipes.

Chef Leslie closed Chez Hélène, and joined Jacques-Imo's, a funky uptown establishment well suited to his flair. He moved on to Pampy's, where he held the highest office in the kitchen.

Hurricane Katrina closed Pampy's and evacuated Chef Leslie to Atlanta, where he retired but was ready to get back to work, until his last meal was served in 2005.

His was the first New Orleans jazz funeral following Katrina. It honored him, parading past restaurants and marching him toward a different heavenly repast. Here on earth you can still get Chef Leslie's stuffed shrimp, if you make them yourself, and you can.

CHEF AUSTIN LESLIE
STUFFED SHRIMP

Stuffed shrimp is about as close to heaven as culinary sins can get. The dressing is wrapped around the shrimp, battered, and fried. Chef Austen Leslie's recipe is the benchmark – a crunchy bite, followed by savory crabmeat, and then tender shrimp. Sclafani's in Metairie used to serve its version with Hollandaise sauce, certainly gilding the lily, but delicious nonetheless.

SERVES: 9

6 tablespoons	butter	2 pounds	crabmeat
4 sprigs	parsley, finely chopped	1-1/2 loaves	French bread
1 rib	celery, finely chopped	1 teaspoon	garlic, finely chopped
1/4 cup	green bell pepper, finely chopped	5 large	eggs
1 teaspoon	thyme	3 pounds	jumbo shrimp, peeled and deveined with fantails intact
1 large	onion, finely chopped	2 cups	all-purpose flour
to taste	salt and freshly ground blackpepper	1-1/2 cups	whole milk
		2 cups	Louisiana Fish Fry or corn flour*
2 teaspoons	Tabasco™ sauce	for frying	vegetable oil

DIRECTIONS

Preheat the oven to 350°F. Melt the butter in a saucepan, add the parsley, celery, bell pepper, thyme, onions, salt and pepper, sauté 10-15 minutes. Lower the heat and add crabmeat, sauté an additional 10-15 minutes.

While the crabmeat sautés, moisten the French bread (it should be wet but not soggy), and mash into small pieces. Season with salt, pepper, and Tabasco™ sauce. Beat 2 eggs in a cup and add to the bread, mix well. Remove the crabmeat from the heat. Combine the crabmeat with the bread and egg mixture. Pour the crabmeat dressing in a 9-inch round baking dish, cover and bake for 1 hour. Stir after the first 30 minutes of cooking. Remove from oven, allow to cool, then place in the refrigerator to completely chill.

Season the shrimp with salt and black pepper to taste. Remove crabmeat dressing from the refrigerator. For each shrimp, place 1 tablespoon of dressing in the palm of your hand, molding the dressing around the shrimp to about 1/8-inch thickness. Roll the dressing around the shrimp. Repeat this process until all of the shrimp have been coated with the dressing. Set aside.

Place the flour in a large mixing bowl. In another bowl whisk the remaining 3 eggs and milk together, to form an egg wash. Place the Fish Fry or corn flour* in a third bowl.

Heat the vegetable oil in a large deep skillet. Dredge each shrimp first in the flour, then in the egg wash, and lastly in the fish fry or corn flour. When the oil is hot, fry the shrimp in batches, until golden brown, about 4 minutes. Do not overcrowd the pot, or the shrimp will be heavy and greasy. Remove shrimp from the skillet with a slotted spoon or tongs and place on paper towels to remove excess oil. Keep the shrimp warm by placing in a warm oven. Serve immediately.

*or finely ground corn meal

HERBSAINT
SHRIMP AND TOMATO BISQUE

Shrimp bisque is Louisiana's answer to the North's lobster version. We, of course, prefer our crustaceans and our recipes. Chef Donald Link adds a wry twist to his recipe with tomatoes, rice for thickening, and a kick of Herbsaint® liqueur.

YIELD: 8 CUPS

2 cups	shrimp, 16-20 count		2 cups	shrimp stock
6 tablespoons	butter		1 cup	water
1 cup	celery, roughly chopped		1/4 cup	white rice, uncooked
3/4 cup	carrot, roughly chopped		4 tablespoons	Herbsaint® liqueur
3/4 cup	white onions, roughly chopped		4 tablespoons	brandy
1 tablespoon	fresh garlic, chopped		to taste	Tabasco™ sauce
1/2 cup	tomatoes, roughly chopped		1 tablespoon	fresh tarragon, chopped
1 cup	canned tomatoes (8 ounces)		to taste	salt and pepper
1 tablespoon	tomato paste		1 cup	heavy cream

DIRECTIONS

Rinse the shrimp well, then peel and remove the back vein. Set aside all the heads and shells. Set aside one shrimp for each serving as garnish to float on top of the soup. Chop the remaining shrimp and refrigerate until ready to use.

To make the shrimp stock, place the shrimp heads and shells in a large pot, and cover with 3 quarts of water. Bring to a boil over high heat, then lower the heat, and simmer gently, until reduced to about 2 quarts.

In a large heavy-bottomed saucepan, melt 4 tablespoons of butter, over low heat. Sauté celery, onions, and carrot, covered, until soft, about 20 minutes. Add the garlic, tomatoes, canned tomatoes, and tomato paste. Mix well and simmer for 5 more minutes.

Add the chopped shrimp, and continue cooking for 20 minutes. Add the shrimp stock and water and bring to a simmer. When the vegetables are completely tender, add the rice, and cook for 15 minutes. Add Herbsaint®, brandy, hot sauce, tarragon, salt and pepper to taste. Sauté or boil the garnish shrimp in a skillet over medium heat for 3-4 minutes. Set aside.

Purée all ingredients in a blender or food processor until very smooth, and pass through a strainer with medium-sized holes. Return the strained bisque to a heavy-bottomed pot over low fire. Stir in the cream, 2 tablespoons of butter, and additional splash of Herbsaint®, brandy, hot sauce, salt and pepper to taste. Toss the reserved shrimp in olive oil.

Serve in soup cups, or wide, shallow soup bowls and garnish with shrimp and chopped parsley.

Note: Herbsaint® liqueur is made primarily in New Orleans. If unavailable, Pernod liqueur may be used as a substitute.

Best Chef South, the prestigious 2007 James Beard Foundation Award, honored Donald Link for his accomplishments at Herbsaint, a tiny bistro named for the New Orleans liqueur. Link has received other major awards, national press, local fans and has made his name in a food-obsessed town.

The corner of Girod and St. Charles is home for an abundance of flavorful dishes. From Acadian roots, Link grew as sous chef with Susan Spicer at Bayona. As partners, they created Herbsaint to showcase his talent. Link, in turn, has opened Cochon with his former sous chef, now co-owner Chef Stephen Stryjewski.

While Spicer's Bayona features an international flavor, Link's Herbsaint takes direction from his Louisiana background. Cochon celebrates county-style cooking, and features a wood burning oven.

Herbsaint's menu offers small plates and appetizers along with entrées. Guests may share several, and then order several more.

We do that happily here in New Orleans.

FINFISH & COMBOS

Somewhere in our development, guys discovered that they needed to grill, and now it's a Y-chromosome thing. If they ever get the chance, women enjoy it, too, perhaps for slightly different reasons.

Seafood, in particular, is partial to grilling outdoors, but it has gotten a bad rap since it can tend to stick to the grill and then under- or over-cook. None of that is a necessity. Clever thinkers have created fish holders, pierced baskets, grill-worthy cast-iron skillets, metal skewers, and wooden planks. Seafood can be smoked, grilled, blackened, baked or skewered.

The thrill of the grill has taken us back outdoors, so we will not smoke up the kitchen, we will not turn on the oven, and we will not make our living space smell like fish. These are X-chromosome things.

Blackened redfish is a magical dish created by Chef Paul Prudhomme. When he acquired the old Austin Inn on Chartres Street and transformed it into world-famous K-Paul's, there wasn't a grill, so he made do with a cast-iron skillet and his special seasoning mix. The result made culinary headlines. Lines formed at his place. New Yorkers lined up when he took K-Paul's from the Big Easy to visit the Big Apple. His celebrity brought Cajun cooking to the forefront of the country, which turned out to be a mixed blessing.

Non-Cajun imitators opened restaurants, slathering their dishes with pepper and spices, burning the devil out of perfectly good fish, steaks, and mouths. Incredible. Inedible. Caveat emptor.

Redfish has been abused. Blackening has developed a bad name, which it does not deserve. Blackened means seasoned and seared, not burned and black. Certainly we use pepper – black, white, cayenne – but to season, not to beat the dish insensible.

The beauty on the facing page is a line-caught, fresh redfish, clear-eyed, glistening, and ready for dinner.

The fish could speak for itself, but we ate it.

The recipe for this redfish, or any other firm fish, is so simple it doesn't need elaboration. Slice the fish belly and gut it, or have your fish monger gut the fish, leaving the scales and skin on. You may have it scaled if you prefer but it doesn't matter.

Stuff the belly cavity with rosemary, thyme, oregano or other herbs of your choice, and tuck in lemon slices. Put the whole fish in the holder and place over a medium hot fire for 8 to 10 minutes and turn, cooking for another 4 to 5 minutes. Test for doneness. The fish may also be grilled for two or three minutes on each side for the smoky flavor then placed in a 400ºF oven for 15 minutes to finish cooking. To serve, split the fish in half from the belly, remove the herbs, and open the fish. Carefully lift out the bone in one piece. The skin will simply slide off.

Chef Reggio, began his career as an apprentice under the late, legendary Chef Warren LeRuth. Greg has developed his own version of this much-maligned recipe by using specific measurements and processes. He has great respect for the freshest and best products. It is simple to create a splendid, beautiful redfish fillet that's flavorful on the outside and tenderly moist on the inside with his recipes and methods.

Greg is one of the Taste Buds, a trio of chefs who have developed ground-breaking restaurants and recipes at Zea Rotisserie, and Semolina's Bistro Italia. Chefs Gary Darling and Hans Limburg are his partners.

In the kitchen, follow the same procedure with the skillet, quickly sear both sides of the fish and place in a 400°F oven for 15 to 20 minutes until it tests done.

Greg swears by Chef Paul Prudhomme's Blackened Redfish-Magic Seasoning Blend™ and the Taste Buds use it for their restaurant recipes. That's good enough for me.

CHEF GREG REGGIO
BLACKENED* REDFISH

Chef Greg Reggio says there are two sensible ways to blacken redfish at home; one outside on the grill, the other inside in the oven. Outside first.

YIELD: 4 FILLETS

4	fresh redfish fillets, 6 to 7 ounces each, 1/2 to 3/4 inches thick, skin off
1 pound	unsalted butter, melted and clarified
5 teaspoons	Chef Paul Prudhomme's Blackened Redfish-Magic Seasoning Blend™
14"	cast-iron skillet, seasoned
1	dish towel
1	fish spatula, long

DIRECTIONS

Over low heat, warm unsalted butter until it melts. Remove from heat and let stand, to allow the milk solids to settle to the bottom. Pour off the clarified butter, put into a container and set aside.

Lightly dust each redfish fillet on both sides with 1 1⁄4 teaspoons of blackened seasoning. Don't overdo it. It should be a thin coating, only a grain or so deep. For bronzed redfish, cut the seasoning amount in half.

Place a seasoned, cast-iron skillet on the grill over a bed of coals, which have developed a light coating of ash, and heat until it is just turns a dull black, no hotter. Red hot is too hot; white hot, if you can even achieve it, is way too hot. If using a gas grill, heat the skillet over a medium high flame. Carefully ladle 2 tablespoons of butter oil into the skillet in the shape of the fillets you plan to place there.

Immediately add the fillets to the pan, rounded side down. This is the presentation side of the fish. Watch carefully as the edges and thin tail begin to cook and turn white, approximately 3-4 minutes. Using a long-blade fish spatula, gently turn the fillets. Cook the flat side another 2-3 minutes. Take care not to overcook. With the tip of a finger, press the thickest part of the fish. If the fingerprint says indented, the fish is done. Remove from grill, place on a warmed plate and brush with a light coating of clarified butter. Serve.

Wipe the skillet in between uses with a kitchen towel, removing any of the spices, bits of fish, and oil. Otherwise the debris will stick to the next fillets, creating a charred taste. Throw away the towel when you are finished.

Redfish on the half shell can be prepared in exactly the same way, by leaving the skin on one side of the fillet and placing the fish directly on the cool side of the grill. Serve the entire fillet on the plate. The meat pulls away from the skin, leaving behind a canoe-shaped charred solid shell.

COCHON RESTAURANT
CATFISH COURTBOUILLON

Chef Link says use any seafood stock for this dish. Traditionally, it is made with fish stock, but shrimp or crawfish stock will work just fine. This recipe was made with a crawfish stock because it happened to be on hand. Do not make this with water; it is not worth the effort. If nothing else, take two whole small fish and chop them, place them in cold water, and bring to a boil. Reduce heat and simmer partially covered for 45 minutes, then strain for a simple stock.

SERVES: 2

1 tablespoon	clarified butter		1/4 teaspoon	paprika
1/2 medium	onion, diced small		1/2 cup	dry white wine
1/2 medium	green bell pepper, diced small		1 cup	fish or shrimp stock
1 medium	jalapeño, serrano or cayenne, diced small		1 pound	catfish fillets
			1/2 cup	all-purpose flour
1 stalk	celery, diced small		1/2 cup	cornmeal
1/2 teaspoon	dried thyme		2 tablespoons	vegetable oil or bacon fat
1 teaspoon	salt		1/4 cup	green onions, chopped
1/4 teaspoon	ground white pepper		1 large	lemon, juiced
1/4 teaspoon	ground black pepper		1/4 cup	parsley, chopped
1/4 teaspoon	cayenne pepper		5	fresh basil leaves
			1 1/2 cups	cooked white rice

DIRECTIONS

In a large heavy-bottomed saucepan, melt butter over medium heat. Add the onions, bell pepper, jalapeño, celery, thyme, salt, peppers, and paprika. Sauté over medium heat for 5 minutes. Add the white wine and cook 10 more minutes until the wine is almost evaporated. Add the seafood stock and cook 5 more minutes. Keep the sauce warm while you sauté the fillets.

Season catfish fillets with salt and pepper to taste. Using a cast-iron pot or a heavy-bottomed skillet, heat the vegetable oil over medium high heat.

In a small shallow pan combine the flour and cornmeal. Coat catfish with the mixture and sauté for 3 minutes on the rounder side. Flip the fish over, add the sauce, then let simmer for 5-8 minutes.

Finish with green onions, lemon juice, parsley, and fresh torn basil leaves. Gently remove the catfish with a slotted spatula and set over rice. Then spoon the sauce generously over the catfish. You may want to serve this in a large bowl so the sauce doesn't splash over the rim.

Chef Stephen Stryjewski and co-owner Chef Donald Link embrace the traditions of southern cooking with passion and joy.

Chef Stephen graduated from the Culinary Institute of America, then, following a tour of restaurants in Europe and Napa Valley, landed in New Orleans. Beginning as a line cook at Herbsaint, he was quickly promoted to sous chef.

After working as a sous chef at Donald Link's Herbsaint, it was time for Stephen to run his own operation. Cochon is a contemporary, casual establishment outfitted with a wood-burning oven and a cheerful wait staff. My only argument is the custom-made chairs. I swear they will wind up as kindling in that oven.

Cochon was nominated in the first year as a James Beard Foundation Best New Restaurant, South.

The James Beard Foundation Awards recognize outstanding achievement within the national food and wine industry and are considered to be the Oscars of the food world.

© Photograph Jeffery Johnston

Chef Chris Kerageorgiou created a serene haven across Lake Pontchartrain named La Provence in honor of his native France. We would hire a car to Lacombe and back so we could enjoy the wine cellar without concern.

Our last visit was an enchanted occasion, as we sipped a crisp, chilled Meursault beside the fireplace as course after course appeared, each more extraordinary. Cooking and visiting with guests were labors of love with Chef Chris.

His appetite for civic and charitable events was generous. He and La Riviera's Chef Goffredo cavorted through special events as a culinary comedy duo.

In 2007, Chef Chris died. La Provence was bought by its sous chef, John Besh, who had graduated to make his own mark as a James Beard Foundation award-winning chef. Besh has a proud legacy to preserve and enhance while making La Provence his own, under a benign spirit's watchful gaze.

CHEF CHRIS KERAGEORGIOU'S
CATFISH FILLET

Remember blind dates when the person setting you up would say that the prospect had a great personality? Consider catfish a blind date. They're so pitifully homely that no one but another catfish would want anything to do with them. As further protection, catfish fins are cutting sharp. These elaborate mean and ugly whiskers disguise the gorgeous white catfish meat hidden beneath it's fearsome exterior.

Chef Chris added a flavorful sauce that enhanced, rather than overpowered the fish. The sparkle of Creole mustard in tandem with tomatoes, the fillet seasoned with fresh herbs, then poached in wine is a taste and texture revelation.

SERVES: 6

6 large	catfish fillets, skin removed		3 large	tomatoes, peeled, seeded, and diced
1 cup	olive oil, divided			
1/4 cup	shallots, minced		2 tablespoons	Creole mustard
1/4 cup	fresh herbs, thyme, basil rosemary, chopped		to taste	salt and freshly ground black pepper
1 tablespoon	black peppercorns, crushed		garnish	green onions, chopped
2 cups	dry white wine			

DIRECTIONS

WHITE WINE MARINADE
Place the catfish fillets on a sheet of plastic wrap, cover with a second sheet. Use a large chef's knife to flatten the fillets. Place the fillets in a large square pan, coated with 1/4 cup of the olive oil. Sprinkle the fish with any combination of fresh herbs, crushed peppercorns, and half of the shallots. Add the remaining olive oil and 1 cup of white wine. Cover and refrigerate for 2-3 hours. The longer the fish marinates, the better the flavor.

Fold the chilled fillets in thirds, with the herbs on the inside. In a 12-inch or larger saucepan, place the fish in one layer. Sprinkle with remaining shallots, and white wine. Bring to a simmer, lower the heat, cover and cook for 7-10 minutes. When the fish begins to flake, its done. Remove catfish from the pan and keep warm.

CREOLE MUSTARD SAUCE
Strain the liquid and reduce by 2/3 over high heat. Add the diced tomatoes and cook for 2 minutes. Reduce the heat to low and stir in the Creole mustard. Do not allow the sauce to boil. Add salt and pepper to taste, cook for 2 more minutes.

Place the catfish on individual serving plates, and top with the Creole mustard sauce, garnish with green onions. Serve with or without cooked white rice, as desired.

CHEF JOHN BESH
CREOLE BOUILLABAISSE

Marseille, France has bragging rights to the creation of bouillabaisse, a hearty soup made from leftover fishermen's catch. Here, we too, make excellent use of any finfish, crustacean, or shellfish in any combination. You're encouraged to substitute any available fresh seafood or add scrubbed clams, mussels, sea scallops, or lobster tails, if you're feeling particularly expansive.

SERVES: 8

SOUP BASE

1/4 cup	vegetable oil or margarine
1/4 cup	all-purpose flour
1 cup	onions, medium chop
1/2 cup	celery, medium chop
2 cloves	garlic, finely chopped
1/4 cup	fresh parsley, chopped
2 1/2 cups	fish stock or substitute*
1 cup	dry white wine
3 large	fresh tomatoes, skinned, undrained and rough chopped
1 tablespoon	fresh lemon juice
1	bay leaf
1/4 teaspoon	kosher salt
1/4 teaspoon	cayenne pepper
1 tablespoon	fresh chopped dill
1 tablespoon	fresh oregano, chopped

SEAFOOD

1 pound	fresh fish fillets: trout, red snapper, catfish or redfish
5 tablespoons	olive oil
1 pint	fresh oysters, shucked
1 pound	peeled deveined shrimp or fresh crawfish tails, or both
1 pound	jumbo lump crabmeat
1 pint	clams or mussels (optional)
1	large lobster, shelled and cut into pieces

*for substitute stock combine 1/2 cup clam juice, and 2 cups of chicken stock

DIRECTIONS

In a large saucepot add the oil or margarine over medium heat. To prepare the roux, slowly blend in flour and stir constantly, until mixture is light brown and releases a nut-like aroma. This must not be left unattended. If it scorches, start over.

Add onions, celery, garlic, parsley, and continue stirring until the vegetables are tender. Gradually stir in stock. Add the remaining ingredients except the seafood. Bring to a boil, and then simmer for 10 minutes.

In a large saucepan, sauté the bite-sized pieces of fish in olive oil, until they are crisp. Set aside.

Add oysters, shellfish, and lobster and simmer for 5 minutes. Add fish and shrimp, and cook for 5 more minutes or until all seafood is done. Add the crabmeat at the last minute very gently to avoid breaking the lumps. Prepare the rouille spread and toasted crostini (*see sidebar*).

Serve immediately in a tureen or individual shallow bowls, garnish with fresh herbs – float rouille on top of the bouillabaisse.

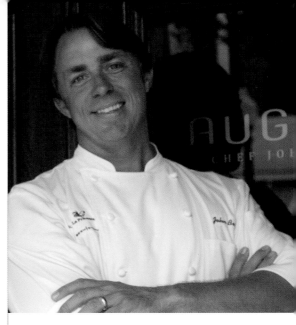

Chef John Besh, who won the James Beard Award for Best Chef of the Southeast in 2006, keeps a full plate. His flagship Restaurant August has consistently been a showcase for the sophisticated side of his creativity.

In early 2007, he purchased the legendary La Provence in Lacombe, Louisiana, from his mentor, Chef Chris Kerageorgiou, for whom he had been a sous chef. There, gardens of herbs and vegetables celebrate the countryside and grace his tables.

Besh's love of the outdoors, hunting, fishing, and bayous underscore his understanding of Louisiana's native cuisine.

ROUILLE SPREAD

1 cup	bread crumbs
2 tablespoons	chimayo chili*
1	garlic clove
3/4 cup	olive oil
1/2 tablespoon	lemon
24	crostini toasts

Pulse in a food processor or blender until smooth enough to spread. Serve with crostini, made of toasted, buttered French or Italian bread.

Under the old oak trees uptown, Lally Brennan and Ti Martin, as managing partners, maintain the grandeur that is Commander's Palace.

James Beard Foundation honored it with the Lifetime Outstanding Restaurant Award; named the late Chef Jamie Shannon Best Chef Southeast region and also honored Commander's with the Outstanding Service Award.

Paul Prudhomme was a former executive chef during Ella, Dick, and Dolly Brennan's long and heralded tenure as proprietors.

This generation continues the family tradition of creativity, quality and service.

GARNISH

1/2 cup	reserved roasted pecans, chopped
6 sprigs	parsley
6	lemon wedges

To serve, place each fillet on the plate, top with a heaping tablespoon of the pecan butter. Cover the entire fillet. Sprinkle with a heaping tablespoon of roasted pecans. Pour the meunière sauce on top and garnish with parsley and lemon wedges.

COMMANDER'S PALACE
Pecan Encrusted Trout

There's nothing more New Orleans than pecans and trout unless it is bringing the tastes together with a drapery of Creole meunière sauce.

SERVES: 6

PECAN BUTTER

1 cup	pecans, shelled		1/2 medium	lemon, juiced
4 tablespoons	unsalted butter, softened		1 teaspoon	Worcestershire sauce

Preheat oven to 350ºF. Spread the pecans on a cookie sheet and bake for 10 minutes. Coarsely chop half of the roasted pecans, and set aside for garnish. Place the remaining pecans into a blender or food processor and finely chop. Add butter, lemon juice, and Worcestershire sauce. Blend into a smooth butter and set aside.

CREOLE MEUNIÈRE SAUCE

2 tablespoons	cooking oil		2 tablespoons	Worcestershire sauce
2 tablespoons	all-purpose flour		1 medium	lemon, juiced
1 1/2 cups	fish stock (recipe p. 83)		1/4 cup	parsley, chopped
8 tablespoons	unsalted butter, cut into cubes and softened		to taste	salt and freshly ground black pepper

Heat the cooking oil in a heavy saucepan. Remove the saucepan from the heat and add flour. Return the pan to the heat and cook, stirring constantly until the roux becomes medium brown in color. Slowly whisk in the fish stock, bring to a boil, stirring constantly, and simmer for 45 minutes. Pour mixture into a 2-quart saucepan and bring to a quick simmer. Add Worcesterhire sauce and whisk in the softened butter cubes one at a time, until the butter is completely incorporated. Add the juice of 1 lemon and parsley. Whisk the sauce briefly, and remove from heat. Keep the sauce warm in the top of a double boiler. Meunière sauce should be used within 45 minutes after completion.

TROUT

2 medium eggs	lightly beaten		1 cup	all-purpose flour
1 cup	milk		6	trout fillets, 6-8 ounces each
2 teaspoons	seafood seasoning (recipe p. 92)		1/2 cup	clarified butter or half cooking oil and half margarine

In a large mixing bowl combine the lightly beaten eggs and milk. Mix well and set aside. In a large pan, combine the Creole seasoning and flour. Place the fillets in the mixture one at a time and coat each fillet very well. Place the coated fish in the egg and milk mixture; return the fish to the seasoned flour mixture for another coating. Melt the clarified butter in a large skillet over medium high heat. Carefully place the fillets in the pan and sauté until golden brown on each side, about 2 minutes per side. Place the crisp fillets onto a warm serving platter. Prepare the garnish (*see sidebar*).

MICHELE VINE
PLANKED FISH

Most objections to grilling fish stem from the flesh sticking to the barbecue grill. I'm fond of my fish shaped wire holder which allows flipping the fish to cook both sides, containing it completely. Another solution is to use an untreated cedar plank, which adds flavor and also provides a nifty serving platter. This method migrated to New Orleans from the Pacific Northwest. We've embraced it and added our local seasonings.

This recipe works well for almost any fresh fish fillet – trout, flounder, redfish, snapper, catfish, drum, tuna, and salmon. To make it even easier, cedar planks for this purpose are packaged and sold for the grill. Preparing them yourself, however, is not what you would call demanding.

This fillet was planked on a bed of lemon balm and oregano, kissed with lemon flavored olive oil then sprinkled with Italian seasoning. It is equally good with Creole seasoning, fresh rosemary, basil,

SERVES: 6

6 fillets	fresh fish, scaled and skinned	4 to 6	untreated cedar shingles or cedar boards, larger than a fillet
2 tablespoons	olive oil or clarified butter	6 bundles	fresh herbs of choice
2 tablespoons	Creole seasonings	6	lemon wedges for garnish
to taste	salt and pepper		

DIRECTIONS

Soak untreated cedar shingles or boards in water for at least 2 hours, preferably overnight.

Build a bank of charcoal on one side of the grill and allow it to burn down, causing a coating of ash. Gas grills should be lighted on one side with the other turned off to create an area with less intense heat.

Brush olive oil on each side of each fillet. Season fillets with a thin coating of Creole seasoning, salt, and pepper. Make a bed of herbs on the planks and place the fish flat side down.

Put the cedar plank on the opposite side of the grill from the coals and cover with the grill's lid for 10 to 12 minutes. If using a gas grill, place the plank on the cooler part of the grill. The thicker the fish fillets, the longer it will take for them to grill.

Do not turn the fish. Press the thickest part of the fillet with your finger. The fish is done when the fingerprint stays indented, or when it begins to flake.

Another method is to place the planked fish on the covered grill for 3-4 minutes to acquire the smoky flavor, then finish cooking on the plank in a preheated 400°F oven for 10-15 minutes. Garnish with lemon wedges, and serve on the plank, or move to a plate immediately.

Note: If the edges of the plank char, it merely enhances the presentation. The planks are reusable after cleaning. Hickory or Maple chips add another flavorful dimension.

Michele Vine, a Renaissance woman in our time, prefers to make things herself, including rebuilding her house. She can take a barbecue pit and dazzle her guests, building a meal from simple ingredients.

Her planked fish recipe is from a happy collaboration with Ernie Dorand, her neighbor. He adds black olives. Michele does not. Nor does she use lumber from her construction site. Ernie gave her a proper unseasoned cedar plank.

She returned home from California following Katrina to help the city and her family. Michele not only assisted in the test kitchen but checked the hundreds of details and edits that a book involves.

If you would like to build a house, or build a book, Michele is your kind of woman.

Antoine's Restaurant
Since 1840

Pompano en Papillote was devised by Jules Alciatore, the second proprietor of Antoine's Restaurant in New Orleans, in honor of the Brazilian balloonist Alberto Santos-Dumont. Antoine's was founded in 1840, America's oldest family-owned restaurant.

Traditionally, a pompano fillet is baked in sealed parchment paper enclosed along with white wine, shrimp, crabmeat, seasonings and colorful vegetables.

An old-fashioned recipe uses a blond roux and egg yolks, creating a liaison, which can curdle and make the result look less than appealing.

The technique is really steaming it in the oven. If you are fortunate in completely sealing the parchment, the enclosure will puff, suggesting a balloon. Cut at the table by each guest, it is a celebration entrée.

Contemporary versions are popular, making use of any variety of fish and vegetables, even chicken breasts. Pompano is recommended, since the fillets are about the same thickness and therefore cook evenly.

ANTOINE'S
POMPANO EN PAPILLOTE

SERVES: 6

3 medium sized	pompanos or 6 fillets	12	cooked shrimp, whole
3 cups	water	1/2 clove	garlic, minced
1	shallot, chopped	1 1/2 cups	onions, chopped
1 tablespoon	parsley, chopped	2 cups	fish stock or clam juice
12	peppercorns	12 sprigs	thyme
1/2	lemon, juiced	36	basil leafs
1	bay leaf	12	whole asparagus
to taste	kosher salt and freshly	1 large	tomato, sliced
6 tablespoons	unsalted butter	2	lemons, thinly sliced
1 cup	lump crabmeat	to taste	ground white pepper
2 1/4 cups	dry white wine		

DIRECTIONS

In a large saucepot, add water, shallots, parsley, peppercorns, lemon juice, bay leaf, and salt. Allow the liquid to simmer over medium heat, about 5 minutes. Add the fillets and simmer over low heat for 5-8 minutes. Remove the fillets from the pan and set aside. Increase the heat and allow the stock to cook over high heat until the liquid is reduced to about 2 cups. Strain the poaching liquid/fish stock and reserve.

In a large 12-inch saucepan melt 2 tablespoons of butter over medium heat. Sauté the crabmeat, shrimp, and garlic in two tablespoons of butter. Add onions, and remaining garlic, cook for 10 minutes. Add thyme, bay leaf, and 1 3/4 cup of fish stock. Simmer for 10 minutes. Remove from heat and set aside. Preheat the oven to 450°F.

In a heavy-bottomed saucepan, melt the remaining 2 tablespoons of butter, over low heat. Add the green onions and cook until softened. Slowly stir in remaining 1/4 cup of fish stock. Add the crabmeat mixture. Simmer, stirring constantly until thickend. Add the remaining white wine, salt, and white pepper to taste. Transfer to a large bowl and allow to cool completely, then chill in the refrigerator, about 1 hour.

Cut parchment paper hearts 12 inches long and eight inches wide. Using clarified butter oil or olive oil, coat the paper well inside and out. Place the basil and thyme in the center of one side of the heart. Place the fillet, topped with the crabmeat and shrimp mixture on the bed of herbs. Add vegetables, asparagus spears, tomato slices, and lemon slices. Fold the other half of the paper over, creating a crescent shape. Close the edges of the paper by folding over and pinching together all around until completely sealed. Lay sealed crescents on an oiled baking sheet and bake at 450°F for 15 minutes, or until paper is browned. Some parchment paper may not brown, but do not cook any longer than 20 minutes. Place on plates and serve at once, cutting open the paper at the table so the steam and aroma escape with an ahhhhh.

REDFISH WITH CRABMEAT AND LEMON BUTTER SAUCE

SERVES: 6

LEMON BUTTER SAUCE

1 1/2 cup	dry white wine
1 teaspoon	cider vinegar
5	lemons, juiced and seeds removed
1/2 teaspoon	lemon zest
1 teaspoon	shallots, minced

1 clove	garlic, minced
4 sprigs	thyme, chopped
2 cups	unsalted butter
1 pinch	kosher salt
1 pinch	black pepper

REDFISH

6-8 ounces	redfish fillets, bone and skin removed
3/4 cup	clarified butter
1 pinch	kosher salt
1 pinch	black pepper
1 cup	flour, seasoned with salt and cayenne pepper to taste

CRABMEAT

1/4 cup	unsalted butter
1/4 cup	dry white wine
1 pound	jumbo lump crabmeat
1 pinch	kosher salt
1 pinch	black pepper

DIRECTIONS

To make the lemon butter sauce, place all ingredients except butter, salt and pepper in a heavy-bottomed saucepan over medium high heat. Allow the mixture to reduce by 1/2, then lower heat to medium. Slowly whisk in the unsalted butter, do not allow the sauce to come to a boil. Once the butter has been whisked in, add the salt and pepper. Set the sauce aside, this sauce should be kept at a temperature of 140°F. If the sauce gets too cold, it may "break", which means the sauce will no longer be emulsified, and the butter will separate from the sauce.

Place a 12-inch sauté pan over a medium high heat and melt the clarified butter. While the pan is getting hot, season fish on both sides with salt and pepper and lightly dust with flour. Once the butter is melted completely and the pan is hot, place the fish belly side down in the pan to sear. When the fish has a nice sear, turn the fish over and sear the other side. Lower the heat to medium and allow the fish to cook approximately 8 minutes. Carefully pour crabmeat out onto a plate. Place a cup of cold water nearby for rinsing fingertips. Gently pick through the crabmeat and remove any shells and cartilage.

Place a 10-inch skillet on medium high heat. Add the butter and white wine to the hot skillet. Once the butter has melted, and the mixture is hot, add the jumbo lump crabmeat, season with salt and pepper. Gently sauté until the crabmeat is piping hot. As much as possible, avoid stirring because it will break up the jumbo lump crabmeat. Place each fish fillet on a serving plate and top with crabmeat. Cover the redfish and crabmeat with 3 tablespoons of lemon butter sauce. Serve warm.

A graduate in 1990 from the Culinary Institute of America in Hyde Park, New York, Executive Chef Gregg Collier's hands-on training found him working with such culinary greats as Emeril Lagasse and Chef Jamie Shannon at Commander's Palace prior to joining the Red Fish Grill.

The Red Fish Grill is another Brennan family establishment, owned and operated by Ralph Brennan. Ralph is also from the Commander's side of the family. Has anyone started counting yet?

Ralph commissioned artist Luis Colemares to create the funky decor, from the bar stools to the hand-painted table tops. Luis works in a feel it, see it, laugh at it kind of manner, perfect for the Redfish Grill concept.

Ralph is a born and bred restaurateur, having proven his abilities at Bacco and Ralph's on the Park. He created each of his new restaurants after taking his turn under Aunt Ella Brennan's watchful eye at Mr. B's Bistro in the French Quarter.

Culinary school is not just for aspiring chefs. Many students are home cooks looking to get better.

Grace Bauer, after raising 4 children and a husband, had earned her status as a superb cook, catering to whims, idiosyncrasies, desires, and diets for her family. She entertains graciously and frequently.

Her adventurous spirit sent her to study at Cordon Bleu and Kitchen Academy. As part of her externship, she worked on this book as a test cook, and with Chef Tommy DiGiovanni in Arnaud's grand kitchens.

Surprisingly enough, or perhaps not surprising at all, her 30 years of experience as one of the county's top commercial interior designers served her well. It gave her the patience, planning, timing, color sense, and creativity necessary to excel in any kitchen.

GRACE BAUER
SEAFOOD TURKEY GUMBO

Seafood gumbo is a family staple that every New Orleans cook approaches with pride and enthusiasm. It's a stovetop forum for creativity. Grace's recipe calls for poultry, leftover turkey, or roasted chicken and some cooks stick strictly to seafood. You're free to use the ingredients that most please you.

SERVES:

1 pound	smoked sausage	1 can	diced tomatoes (15 ounces)
2 pounds	shrimp, peeled and deviened	1 tablespoon	garlic, finely chopped
1 pound	turkey meat, shredded	2	bay leaves
5 to 7	Louisiana blue crabs, cleaned	1 tablespoon	fresh thyme, chopped
1 pint	Gulf oysters (optional)	1/2 cup	flat leaf parsley, chopped
5 tablespoons	bacon drippings or oil	1/8 teaspoon	cayenne pepper
1 cup	olive or vegetable oil	2 teaspoons	ground black pepper
1 cup	all-purpose flour	2 teaspoons	salt
2 cups	onions, finely chopped	2 teaspoons	Creole seasonings (recipe p. 92)
1 1/2 cups	celery, finely chopped	1 cup	fresh okra
1 cup	green bell pepper, chopped	4 cups	shrimp or fish stock
1/2 cup	green onions, chopped (white and green parts)	6 cups	turkey or chicken stock
		6 to 8 cups	cooked white rice

DIRECTIONS

Cut the sausage in 1/4-inch slices, and brown in a large gumbo pot. Deglaze the pot with 2 cups of chicken stock. Add the shrimp stock and diced tomatoes. Allow to simmer over low heat.

Sauté the onions, celery, and bell peppers in a heavy skillet in 3 tablespoons of bacon drippings or oil, for about 8-10 minutes. When the onions are translucent, add the green onions, garlic, parsley, and cook for 3-5 minutes more. Add thyme, parsley, cayenne, black pepper, salt, and Creole seasonings. Transfer the vegetables to the soup or gumbo pot.

Prepare a medium-dark colored roux. Once the roux has been started, it must not be left unattended. It must be stirred constantly, scraping the sides and bottom of the pan to prevent sticking or scorching. In a clean saucepan add 1 cup of oil, over low heat. When the oil is hot, slowly add the flour, stirring constantly, until the roux is the color of chocolate, about 30-45 minutes. When the roux is the desired color, slowly add 1 cup of warm chicken stock and mix well. Carefully add the roux mixture to the soup or gumbo pot. Add the remaining chicken stock and mix well. Simmer for about 20 minutes.

In a clean saucepan, sauté the okra in 2 tablespoons of bacon drippings over low heat. Stir occasionally, and cook until the okra is no longer ropey, about 20 minutes.

Break the crabs in half, add to the gumbo pot, increase the heat, and bring to a boil. Reduce the heat, cover the pot, and simmer. After cooking for about 30 minutes add the shrimp, and oysters (optional). Simmer, covered, for about 20 minutes more. Taste and adjust seasonings, as desired. Serve over cooked white rice.

REMOULADE
SEAFOOD JAMBALAYA

We make jambalaya from just about anything. This recipe honors seafood and andouille sausage. If seafood is not available, use chicken. If andouille sausage is difficult to come by, replace it with smoked sausage. It's hard to go wrong. One final note. Andouille sausage is spicy, so don't add the seasoning until the end, when you may desire a little more kick, but chances are it is already there.

SERVES: 6

FISH STOCK

1 pound	fish trimmings		1	dried thyme
1/2 cup	shallots, chopped		1	bay leaf
1/2 leek	leek, chopped		6	black peppercorns
1/2 cup	celery, chopped		1/2 cup	white wine
1 pinch	fresh parsley, chopped		3 quarts	water

JAMBALAYA

2 tablespoons	vegetable oil		1	bay leaf
1/2 pound	seasoned, smoke sausage such as andouille, diced		1 teaspoon	thyme, crushed
			1/8 teaspoon	cayenne pepper
2 cloves	garlic, finely chopped		1/2 teaspoon	kosher or sea salt
1/2 cup	green onions, chopped		1 1/2 cups	fish stock
1 cup	green bell pepper, chopped		1 cup	long grain rice, uncooked
1/4 cup	fresh parsley, chopped		2 pounds	jumbo shrimp, peeled and deveined
1 1/2 cups	canned tomatoes with liquid, chopped			

DIRECTIONS

Rinse the fish trimmings in cold water several times. Place the trimmings with the vegetables and seasonings in a 2-gallon pot, then add the wine and the water and bring to a boil. Reduce the heat and simmer for 15 minutes. Remove from the heat, skim, and allow to cool. Strain the liquid and store in an airtight container.

Note: Fish stock can be kept in the refrigerator for 3-4 days, or can be successfully frozen.

In an 2-gallon, heavy-bottomed pot or Dutch oven with a tight-fitting lid, warm the oil over medium-low heat. Sauté the sausage, about 3 minutes, until warmed through. Stir in the garlic, green onions, and green bell pepper. Cook until tender, stirring occasionally, about 7-10 minutes.

Add the parsley, tomatoes, bay leaf, thyme, cayenne pepper, salt, fish stock, and rice. Stir the mixture thoroughly, then add the shrimp. Bring to a boil, reduce the heat to very low and cover the pot tightly. Cook without stirring (or transfer to 350°F oven) for 25-30 minutes or until the rice is fluffy. Remove the bay leaf and fluff the rice with a fork. Garnish with parsley leaves and serve immediately.

Remoulade is a handsome antique oyster bar that celebrates fresh Louisiana seafood along with a fine selection of local dishes. Next door to Arnaud's, it stands as the grande dame's nod to casual Creole cooking.

While Orleanians dine extravagantly on occasion, we also relish a great plate of jambalaya, red beans and rice, gumbo, fresh seafood, and other more casual concoctions stirred up in local kitchens.

Rice is a staple in these dishes; many are served for large gatherings. It is this kind of Creole pot food cooking that we all enjoy at home.

Remoulade is named in honor of Arnaud's famous sauce and offers a few of its big sister's specialties such as Oysters Arnaud and Shrimp Arnaud.

The decor is cheerful and the exposed brick reminds us that it is one of the French Quarter's original Creole homes. Artist Luis Cogley created Remoulade's signature metal sculptures.

Sometimes nothing but a seafood pan roast will satisfy. That's when we head to Pascal's Manale. Everyone has a private version, and this one was provided from the home-kitchen friendly Chef Mark DeFelice. It is a high tolerance recipe, which means that there's not much you can do to hurt it, unless you overcook it. The DeFelice family would be unhappy if you did that.

Founded in 1913, this family-run, Italian-Creole restaurant is located in uptown New Orleans and is most famous for creating B-B-Q shrimp. The exact Manale recipe is, of course, a family secret. Secret recipes seem to run in family restaurants.

Pascal's Manale is vintage New Orleans, from the service to the decor. The wait staff is familiar. They're friends of the patrons and know what regulars will order.

Out front, the cocktail lounge and old-time oyster bar is the place to wait for a table. Inside the dining room, dishes such as B-B-Q shrimp, Italian specialties, and New Orleans seafood are worth the wait.

PASCAL'S MANALE RESTAURANT
SEAFOOD PAN ROAST

Pascal's Manale is one of the city's favorite old-fashioned restaurants. Not much here changes, and we like that. Generations of families have made it their traditional Thursday night treat, and it's no wonder. Thursday used to be the cook's night off, if your family was fortunate enough to have a cook. If your family didn't have a cook, mom appreciated the break. Everyone appreciates it so much that most evenings the restaurant is packed.

SERVES: 8

1 pound	butter	1 quart	oysters, chopped
2 medium	onions, finely chopped	1 pound	shrimp, peeled and deveined
2 medium	green bell pepper, finely chopped	1 pound	lump crabmeat
1 bunch	curly parsley, finely chopped	to taste	salt and white pepper
2 bunches	green onions, finely chopped	1 1/2 cups	Italian bread crumbs
1 to 2 quarts	oyster liquor or shrimp stock	to taste	Tabasco™ sauce
4 cups	all-purpose flour	1 loaf	French bread

DIRECTIONS

In a heavy-bottomed saucepan, melt the butter over medium heat. Add the onions, bell peppers, parsley, green onions, and cook vegetables until very tender, approximately 10-12 minutes.

Preheat the oven to 350°F.

Rinse the shrimp with cold water. Pour the crabmeat out onto a plate and remove any shells. Add the shrimp and oysters to the pan, and cook for 5-7 minutes. Fold in the flour a little at a time with a spoon until thoroughly incorporated. The mixture will be thick, add small amounts of the oyster liquor or shrimp stock, continuing to fold in, until a creamy texture is reached. Bring to a simmer, add the crabmeat and season with salt, white pepper, and Tabasco™ sauce to taste.

Pour the mixture into a 2-quart baking dish or individual ramekins. Spread the bread crumbs on top and bake for approximately 15 minutes or until the bread crumbs have browned.

Serve with warm French bread.

CHEF TOM COWMAN
TROUT MOUSSE WITH DILL SAUCE

The late Chef Tom Cowman at Restaurant Jonathan made this canapé or appetizer popular in the early 80s. This version is simplified for the home kitchen and can be molded into a fish shape or in a small loaf pan then upturned onto a pretty bed of greens. The sauce relies on fresh dill to achieve its maximum potential. Use dried dill if you must, but the fresh taste difference is remarkable. If dried dill is used, cut the amount in half since dried herbs are much more flavor intensive. Crostini or crackers should be served alongside the mousse for easy scooping.

SERVES: 12-16

POACHING STOCK

4 cups	water
1 cup	dry sherry
1	medium onion, roughly chopped
3 ribs	celery, roughly chopped
1	bay leaf
1 teaspoon	salt
1/2 teaspoon	white pepper

DILL SAUCE

1 cup	mayonnaise
2-3 tablespoons	fresh dill minced
1 tablespoon	Creole mustard
1/2 teaspoon	onion powder
6 drops	Tabasco™ sauce
1 tablespoon	lemon juice

TROUT MOUSSE

1 pound	trout fillets (flounder, catfish or sole fillets can be substituted)
1 cup	mayonnaise
1 tablespoon	lemon juice
2 tablespoons	Dijon mustard
1/2 teaspoon	Tabasco™ sauce
1 teaspoon	tarragon leaves, chopped
1 teaspoon	dill weed, finely chopped
2 packages	gelatin, unflavored
1 tablespoon	onions, grated
1/2 teaspoon	onion powder
1/2 teaspoon	salt
1 cup	poaching stock

Restaurant Jonathan was the epitome of chic. Women were elegant and men swaggered beside them. A sophisticated cocktail lounge led into a dining room well suited for the smart see-and-not-be-seen haven. It was just down the street from the more casual Marti's on North Rampart on the edge of the French Quarter.

Architect turned restaurateur Jack Cosner fluffed and buffed the old Creole townhouse into an Art Deco jewel, flashing Erté artwork, etched glass, palm trees and other period accoutrements. Celebrities would jet in for a quiet, uninterrupted dinner. Privacy was de rigueur.

Michael Wynne Morris followed Jack Cosner as proprietor, and continued the drama that was Restaurant Jonathan until extended street repairs on North Rampart caused a final curtain call. Chef Tom Cowman, with fans following him, moved uptown to the Upperline. In New Orleans, a great chef always has a second act.

DIRECTIONS

In a large saucepan, combine water, sherry, onions, celery, bay leaf, salt, and pepper. Boil for 15 minutes to create the poaching stock. Remove from heat and allow to cool. Place the fish in a shallow pan and pour the cooled stock over the fish, covering the fish completely. Bring the liquid to a simmer over a low fire. Poach the fish for approximately 7-10 minutes or until it flakes easily. Strain the liquid and reserve for the purée and to dissolve the gelatin.

Prepare the dill sauce by combining all ingredients, mix well, and refrigerate.

Place the fish in a food processor, adding approximately 1/3 cup or just enough poaching liquid to create a textured, moist purée. Stir in the mayonnaise, lemon juice, mustard, Tabasco™ sauce, tarragon, and dill. Sprinkle the gelatin over 1 cup of cold poaching liquid, let stand for 1 minute to bloom. In a small saucepan, heat the gelatin mixture until completely incorporated. Spray a quart-sized fish mold or loaf pan with cooking oil spray. Fill the pan with mousse and refrigerate overnight or until firm. Carefully unmold the mousse and using a wet paring knife, slice into 3/4 inch slices. Serve with crostini, made of toasted, buttered French or Italian bread.

The amount of effort that goes into a seafood boil is such that seafood shops and markets do a fine business selling already boiled carry-out feasts.

If you want to make your own, seafood markets are also happy to fillet your fish selections, clean the soft shell crabs and let you know when the crawfish and shrimp are due hot out of the pot.

Cover the table with black plastic garbage bags, then top them with several layers of newspaper. Dump the drained boil on the table. Cleanup is simple. Stuff the shells and newspapers in the garbage bags you started with.

On Good Friday, the day before the Easter weekend, the entire city goes seafood silly. This could be due to the large Catholic community's tradition of not eating meat on Good Friday, but it has spread to the general population.

Plan to be in line early and plan to wait.

BOILED SEAFOOD

Seafood is usually boiled outside, unless it is a small amount of shrimp or a few crabs for dinner, then it is boiled in the kitchen. A large 10-15 gallon pot allows seafood plenty of room to tumble through the seasoned water. A free standing burner that uses bottled propane is available at hardware and home supply stores. You'll need that, and a backyard.

For seasoning the feast some cooks swear by liquid crab boil. Others only use the traditional dry mix in bags. We each add our own special ingredients to the mix. The most important is personal preference. Also into the boil may go small new potatoes, corn on the cob, links of hot sausage, baby artichokes, lemons, garlic, and even pork tenders.

Crabs and crawfish must be alive when they are added to the boiling water. Before boiling, purge the crabs or crawfish in a large tub of cold water and add half a box of salt. The salt makes them expel any mud or impurities. Allow the crabs or crawfish to rest in the salted water for 10-15 minutes. Change the water by flushing the tub with running water from a garden hose until clear.

CRABS: Allow 6 per person
CRAWFISH: Allow 5 pounds per person
SHRIMP: Allow 2 pounds per person

2 pounds	salt
6 bags	Louisiana shrimp or crab boil
10 whole	garlic heads
6 large	lemons, halved
2 bunches	celery, with leaves
10	bay leaves
2 ounces	black peppercorns
4 pounds	onions, peeled and halved
5 pounds	small whole red potatoes, unpeeled
24 ears	corn, shucked, cut in half or thirds
1/2 pound	cayenne pepper, optional
40 pounds	Louisiana crawfish (serves 12-15 people)

Fill the pot with water to the halfway mark and set over high heat. Add the boil mix, seasonings, and vegetables. Once the water begins to boil add the potatoes and corn. Cook for 10 minutes.

Add the seafood, the water will stop boiling. Put the lid on and allow to return to a boil. When the water starts to boil, begin monitoring the cooking time. Shrimp are ready in about 2-3 minutes, 3-5 for crawfish, and 8-12 minutes for crabs. Do not overcook.

If you overcook the shrimp or crawfish, the shells will stick and peeling will be difficult. When done, remove the pot from the burner and allow the seafood to soak in the seasoned water.

Add 1 or 2 trays of ice cubes to the pot. The ice forces the seafood to the bottom of the pot, to rest in the seasonings. The longer the seafood soaks, the more seasoning they will absorb. Begin testing for flavor after 30 minutes. For spicier seafood, increasing the soaking time. If you can wait that long.

FRIED SEAFOOD

Come fry with me. Seafood likes to be fried. I believe this. The same way I believe a fried shrimp is every bit as good for me as a grilled one. After all, eating fried seafood makes me happy, and isn't being happy good for you?

I'm not suggesting you always fry your fish – or oysters or clams or shrimp or crabs – but I am suggesting that you do so from time to time, and when one of those times strikes, just do it; don't be afraid! You'd be amazed at the number of otherwise normal people today who suffer from Fear of Frying. They think it's complicated.

Bah. Frying seafood is simple, cheap, basic – and safe. They do it all over the world, every day. And why? Because frying is a terrific way to cook almost anything that comes out of the water. You get your crispy on the outside and your moist on the inside. What could be better?

There's no one right way to fry seafood. You can bread it with seasoned cornmeal – or flour (or a combination of the two) or dry bread crumbs, cornstarch or even, believe it or not, crushed Saltines.

Use vegetable oil, butter, olive oil, lard, or a combination, although my own feeling is that when I do, I do it right. Put another way, I use lard. As God intended.

You can marinate or brine your seafood before frying it, or not. You can dip it in an egg or milk batter, or not. Or you can switch back and forth, alternately dipping your pieces of fish – or oysters or shrimp or clams or crabs – in a wet mixture and then a dry mixture. The point is, when it comes to frying seafood, you can go plain or fancy, but if you follow just a few basic rules, what you can't go is wrong.

Use a sturdy pot; the heavier the pot, the better the frying. For me that means a well-seasoned cast-iron skillet (eBay is a great source for these, as are tag sales). But any heavy pot will do. If you're deep-frying, you want a pot with deep sides, and when you pour in the oil (or melt the lard), it should never come higher than half-way up the sides.

You want newspaper or paper grocery bags for draining. It beats the devil out of paper towels, and, no, I don't know why, but it does.

A note on safety: In the Middle Ages, when the invading hordes laid siege to a castle, its defenders poured boiling oil on them. All these years later, boiling oil still burns. So use common sense when frying. Monitor the heat and the oil, don't stand too close to the pot, don't drop things into the oil from a great height, and keep children and pets away from the stove. Beyond that, just relax, pour yourself an adult beverage of your choice, and go fry or grill something that used to swim!

SEAFOOD SEASONINGS
YIELD: 1/2 CUP

2 tablespoons	granulated garlic
2 tablespoons	granulated onions
2 tablespoons	freshly ground black pepper
1 teaspoon	dried oregano
1/2 teaspoon	dried thyme
1/2 teaspoon	white pepper
1/4 teaspoon	dried basil
1/4 teaspoon	cayenne pepper

In a medium sized mixing bowl, mix dry ingredients together using a fork or place in jar, cover and shake thoroughly. Store in a tightly sealed container.

SEASONED FLOUR
YIELD: 2 1/4 Cups

2 cups	all-purpose flour
4 tablespoons	paprika
1 tablespoon	kosher or sea salt
1 tablespoon	garlic powder
1/2 tablespoon	freshly ground black pepper
1/2 cup	cayenne pepper

In a medium sized mixing bowl, mix dry ingredients together using a fork or place in jar, cover and shake thoroughly. Store in a tightly sealed container.

CREOLE SEASONINGS*
YIELD: 1/2 cup

3 tablespoons	sweet paprika
2 tablespoons	onion powder
2 tablespoons	garlic powder
2 tablespoons	dried oregano leaves
2 tablespoons	dried sweet basil
1 tablespoon	dried thyme leaves
1 tablespoon	freshly ground black pepper
1 tablespoon	freshly ground white pepper
1 tablespoon	cayenne pepper
1 tablespoon	kosher or sea salt
dash	chili powder
dash	cumin powder

In a medium sized mixing bowl, mix dry ingredients together using a fork or place in jar, cover and shake thoroughly. Store in a tightly sealed container.

*For Blackened seasoning add an additional tablespoon each of paprika and cayenne pepper.

SEAFOOD FRY
YIELD: 2 1/4 cups

1 cup	corn flour (or finely ground corn meal)
1 cup	all-purpose flour
3 tablespoons	Creole seasoning
1 tablespoon	kosher or sea salt

In a medium sized mixing bowl, mix dry ingredients together using a fork or place in jar, cover and shake thoroughly. Store in a tightly sealed container.

GRILLING SHRIMP

1 pound	shrimp, peeled & deveined
1/4 cup	olive oil
2 tablespoons	Dijon mustard
1/4 cup	fresh dill, finely chopped
1 clove	garlic, minced
1/4 cup	lemon juice
1/2 medium	lemon peel, grated
to taste	kosher or sea salt
to taste	freshly ground black pepper

Preheat the charcoal or gas grill to 400°F.

Place all ingredients in a bowl and mix well. Place the shrimp in a shallow pan and cover with the marinade. Cover and refrigerate for at least 2 hours. Put the shrimp on wooden or metal skewers with or without vegetables. If using wooden skewers, soak in water 20 minutes before using. Place the shrimp on a hot grill and baste with the marinade. Grill the shrimp about 2 minutes per side. For a sweet glaze add 1 or 2 tablespoons of honey, just prior to basting.

GRILLING FISH

1 cup	dry white wine
1/2 cup	olive oil
2 tablespoon	green onions, finely chopped
2 tablespoons	parsley, finely chopped
1 teaspoon	fresh oregano, chopped
1 clove	garlic, minced
1 teaspoon	lemon peel, grated
to taste	salt and ground black pepper
dash	Tabasco™ sauce (optional)

Preheat the charcoal or gas grill to 400°F.

Place all ingredients in a bowl and mix well. Place the seafood in a shallow pan and cover with the marinade. Cover and refrigerate for 2 or more hours, turning occasionally. Place the fish on a hot grill skin side down. Cover and cook over medium heat, until the fish begins to flake. Baste the fish often.

GRILLING SAUCE

1 cup	unsalted butter
1 teaspoon	fresh rosemary, finely chopped
1 teaspoon	fresh tarragon, finely chopped
1 teasppon	fresh basil, torn
2 tablespoons	lemon juice
to taste	kosher salt
to taste	ground white pepper

Preheat the charcoal or gas grill to 400°F.

In a heavy-bottomed saucepan, melt the butter over low heat. Add the fresh herbs, salt and pepper to taste. Add the lemon juice and taste. Adjust seasonings as desired. The sauce should be brushed on before, and during grilling. Basting occasionally. Warm any remaining sauce and use as a dipping sauce.

GRILLING CAJUN STYLE

1 whole	fresh fish
2 teaspoons	lemon pepper seasoning
2 teaspoons	freshly ground white pepper
2 teaspoons	Creole seasoning (recipe p. 92)
1 teaspoon	blackened fish seasoning (recipe p. 92)
1 clove	garlic, minced
4 tablespoons	fresh lemon juice
for fish basket	vegetable cooking spray
4-6 springs	fresh parsley, for garnish
6	lemon weges, for garnish
1	whole redfish, catfish, or flounder

Preheat the charcoal or gas grill to 400°F.

In a small mixing bowl combine the lemon pepper, white pepper, Creole seasoning, and blackened fish seasoning. Rinse the fish well. Sprinkle the fish with lemon juice on both sides. Sprinkle the seasoning mixture on both sides. Spray a wire fish basket with cooking spray and place the fish inside. Grill the fish, covered, over medium coals for 7 to 10 minutes on each side or until the fish begins to flake. Remove fish from the basket and place on a serving platter. Garnish with fresh parsley and lemon wedges.

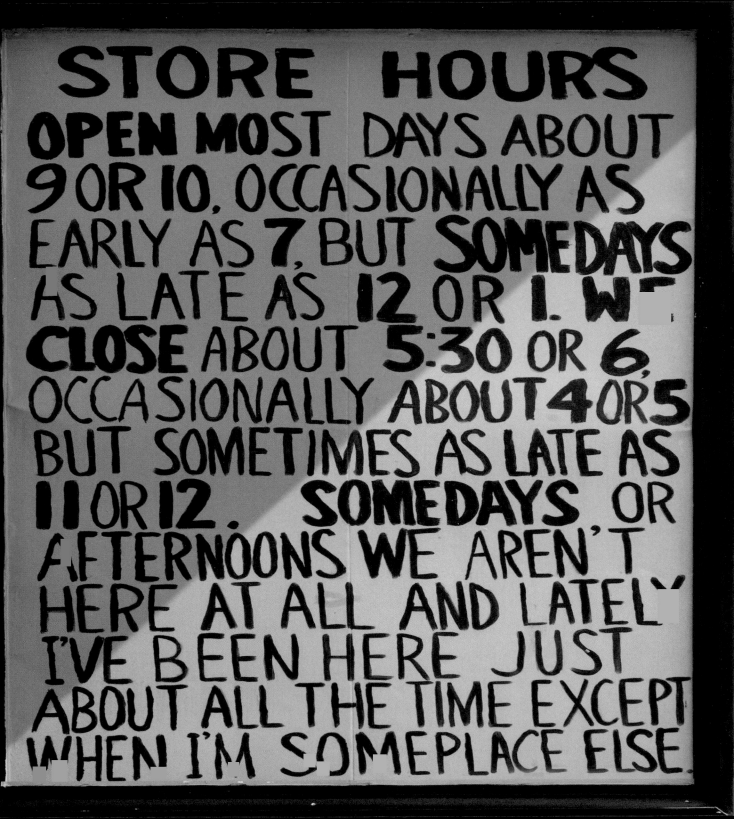

STORE HOURS

OPEN MOST DAYS ABOUT 9 OR 10, OCCASIONALLY AS EARLY AS 7, BUT SOME DAYS AS LATE AS 12 OR 1. WE CLOSE ABOUT 5:30 OR 6, OCCASIONALLY ABOUT 4 OR 5 BUT SOMETIMES AS LATE AS 11 OR 12. SOME DAYS OR AFTERNOONS WE AREN'T HERE AT ALL AND LATELY I'VE BEEN HERE JUST ABOUT ALL THE TIME EXCEPT WHEN I'M SOMEPLACE ELSE.

INDEX

Some products may not be available in all areas. The internet provides a wealth of New Orleans and Louisiana specialties such as Steen's® Cane Syrup and Cane Vinegar. Many seafood companies also ship for next day delivery.